The
Four Corners
of the World

Written & Illustrated by Roger Duvoisin

1948 · NEW YORK ALFRED · A · KNOPF

THIS IS A BORZOI BOOK,
PUBLISHED BY ALFRED A. KNOPF, INC.

THE
FOUR CORNERS OF THE WORLD

THE UNBELIEVABLE ADVENTURE

OF

Francisco Pizarro

CONTENTS

The Swineherd   9

The Poisoned Arrows   11

Six Suns' Journey to the South   19

The Planters and the Priest   27

Hunger in the Swamps:
    First Voyage   33

The Town on the River of Emerald:
    Second Voyage   39

The Lonely Rock   51

CONTENTS

The Flowers of Gold: Third Voyage   61

The King of Spain is Pleased   73

The Four Corners of the World:
    The Conquest   85

One Against Two Thousand   95

Atahuallpa   109

Map   127

Glossary   128

Important Years In Pizarro's Life   128

The Swineherd

Long ago, there lived in the Spanish village of Trujillo a little boy swineherd whose name was Francisco Pizarro. No one cared for him or ever taught him to read or write, and he was so poor that his clothes were all tattered.

Francisco did not like guarding pigs, which he was forced to do to earn his meagre food. He wanted to be a soldier. But, since he was too young for that, too young to go away alone into the big world, he did the next best thing; he dreamed. For long hours he dreamed, sitting on an old wall or lying in the shade of an olive tree.

Sometimes he was a proud soldier with glittering armor over his chest, a steel helmet on his black hair, and a sharp sword by his side, and he was galloping away on his fiery horse while the people of Trujillo waved goodbye in admiration . . .

Sometimes he was a feared captain on a ship sailing faraway seas . . . Or a bold conqueror who landed in an unheard-of country and put to flight the yellow men who lived in houses of gold.

The more Francisco dreamed of adventure the more he disliked being a swineherd. One day he could bear it no longer.

9

He ran away. Although he was only fourteen years of age and barely strong enough to carry the sword and halberd, he joined the King's armies to learn how to become a valiant soldier.

When he was twenty years old, Francisco heard the news of Columbus' voyage across the Atlantic Ocean. What a wonderful tale the courier told! And how the man embellished it as he repeated it again and again!

"That sailor from Genoa," he said, "has just discovered the richest land on earth beyond the mighty ocean; cities of gold, mountains of jewels, people dressed in silk with gold and precious stones all over them. And what strange brown men, beautiful birds and plants, he has brought back! He is already making preparations for another voyage. Let those who care for adventures, glory, and gold, follow him."

"It is just what I had been dreaming about," sighed Francisco when he heard that. "How I wish I could sail in one of Admiral Columbus' ships and come back full of riches and glory. Perhaps I will do so when I end my present service."

Francisco Pizarro's wish was a long time in coming true.

After many, many years had gone by he was still a poor foot soldier bravely fighting in the armies of his King. But he had not lost hope that he would someday sail to America and become a famous conquerer.

The Poisoned Arrows

One day, Francisco Pizarro was strolling along the wharves of Cadiz where so many sailing ships were moored, when he saw a crowd of soldiers and sailors working busily around three fine new ships that swung at anchor. Some soldiers were leading unwilling horses up a gangplank, others were carrying bundles of arquebuses and crossbows, while sailors and Negro helpers plodded up the gangplanks with casks of food and water on their backs.

"Whose ships are these?" Pizarro asked a sailor.

"They are Captain Alonso Ojeda's, a famous captain as everyone knows," answered the sailor. "He is about to sail—to conquer the new countries across the Atlantic Ocean. If you like adventure, soldier, here is your chance. Captain Ojeda needs wise and experienced soldiers like you."

"Ah," exclaimed Pizarro, "this is what I have been waiting for since my youth. All these years I have been dreaming of glorious adventures in the new lands across the ocean. It is there that a brave soldier can find fortune. I'll join your Captain's company indeed, and when I return to Spain I'll be a famous captain myself."

11

"Who can tell?" said the sailor. "Some soldiers have returned from there as poor as when they left; many, many, have not come back at all and now lay buried in some wild forest. But some, like our Captain Ojeda, have returned famous. You may be among the lucky ones. Go and see the Captain, he is the tall man with the plumed helmet up there on the high deck."

"I will," said Pizarro. And he climbed up onto the ship. Any captain would have been proud to include a soldier like Pizarro in his company. He was tall and broad-shouldered, and he wore his steel armor and plumed hat as haughtily as a nobleman; his hair and his beard were graying now, for he was nearly forty years of age, but the daring sparkle in his black eyes told of the courage and the determination that were in him. So, when Captain Ojeda saw this soldier come upon the deck, he hired him at once to join his little company.

And so it was that Francisco Pizarro at last met his chance to embark upon a ship bound for America.

Some days later, he watched with excitement from the railing of his ship the last preparations for the voyage; the last water cask was brought on board, the last cow and pig driven into the holds. And with joyous anticipation, when the anchors were weighed, he joined his soldier comrades in waving his cap to the crowd gathered on the wharf for the sailing.

One by one, the sails spread from their yards, and with a good wind that sang in their riggings, the three ships turned their round prows toward the west.

The wind remained so friendly all the way across the Atlantic Ocean, that less than a month later, Pizarro could see over the prow of his own ship the island of Haiti where Columbus'

ship, the *Santa Maria*, was broken on a rock. Haiti was now a prosperous land, with growing plantations and harbors as busy with ships as any Spanish ports. Captain Ojeda remained there long enough to refill his water casks, take on food and hire more men. Then he led his ships across the Caribbean sea toward the southern land of the Gulf of Darien where he hoped to find a good place to build a new Spanish town.

One morning, when the sun had just risen over the three ships, Pizarro saw a jungle country ahead, greener than any land he had seen. The trees grew right down to the shore and were higher than the mightiest steeples of Spain; the ground under them was like the floor of a green-windowed cathedral. And they were so festooned with lianas that it seemed as if a giant had come to lay his nets to catch the parrots and the monkeys.

When the soldiers landed, the parrots screamed and the monkeys fled. But, hidden in the underbrush, brown Indians crouched in wait with their bows and poisoned arrows. They knew that the bearded men in their shining armor had come to take their land away from them, and to loot their gold jewelry. Whizzing arrows warned Captain Ojeda that the jungle country would not be easily conquered.

"Bah," he said, "our arquebuses will frighten these wild creatures and drive them into their deep forest. Then we shall build our town unhindered."

But his soldiers looked in vain for the elusive Indians. Every day, while the Spaniards tried to cut down trees with which to build a fort, more arrows streaked toward them and more men died. Pizarro's armor was dented by twenty-four arrows.

Captain Ojeda was struck in the leg and to save his life he had to burn his wound with an iron reddened in the fire.

"I would rather fight abroad with the Moors and their flashing swords than be killed by these arrows," said Pizarro. "How can one fight an enemy one does not see?"

He and Captain Ojeda were too courageous to be frightened, but most of their comrades wanted to sail away. They refused to go into the forest to search for food when their provisions had given out.

Fearing that they would starve, Captain Ojeda said to them: "We shall never win this land if we do not have enough food to last until we can build a town, and enough soldiers to fight the Indians. I shall take one ship and go to fetch food and men from the nearest Spanish port. In the meanwhile, you Francisco Pizarro, my bravest soldier, will take command of the men who remain here. If I do not return at the end of fifty days you shall leave on the other two ships."

Captain Ojeda wished good luck to his men and departed.

Thus Francisco Pizarro became a commander at last. He was proud of his little army, even though it looked but like a crowd of beggars—a crowd which became smaller and smaller as the days passed, for the arrows still whistled through the forest.

The allotted fifty days went by and Captain Ojeda did not return. So Pizarro prepared to sail. But, alas, the ships had been so knocked about by the winds and the waves that their old planks could barely keep the sea from pouring into their holds. They could no longer carry safely all the soldiers that were left.

"Since we cannot all leave," said some men, "we must draw lots to decide who will sail and who will stay."

"No," said Pizarro, "that will not do. Those who lose will refuse to stay behind alone in this jungle. I think we will wait a little longer. He thought sadly, "That is the only way. Soon the poisoned arrows and hunger will have made us few enough for the ships to carry."

Every day, Pizarro counted his men, and every day he had less to count. Sometimes an arrow would strike a man down; sometimes hunger or disease would so weaken another that he died.

And Pizarro went on counting his men.

When thirty more days had thus passed, the captain saw

that they could now embark upon the creaky ships. "Make ready" he said then. "Tomorrow at dawn we shall say goodbye to our dead comrades and we shall leave this place."

The next morning, as the ships disappeared over the horizon, the Indians came out of their forest to dance at the edge of the sea. If the Spaniards were glad to sail away, the Indians were even happier to have saved their jungle homes—at least for the present.

However, the adventurers were not at the end of their troubles, for the sea was not less dangerous than the jungle. One of the ships struck a hidden rock and broke into pieces. All on board were drowned. The other ship, which Pizarro commanded, alone arrived at Cartagena, a Spanish port on the Caribbean Sea.

Thus ended Pizarro's first adventure in America.

Six Suns' Journey
to the South

Despite his misfortune Pizarro had not lost heart. Honor and fame still could be his.

He hardly had time to rest and recover from hunger and weariness when a Spanish commander, named Enciso, asked him to join his fleet of sailing ships for a new conquering adventure. And soon Pizarro was back sailing upon the sea, pacing the decks of his same creaky ship with the same old comrades.

The new commander too led his ships toward the green jungle, toward the land of the poisoned arrows and anchored there despite the angry protests of Pizarro's men. It was not long before the arrows flew fiercely again among the adventurers. So many of them fell day after day that the Spaniards threatened to revolt and sail back to a Spanish port. Fortunately a tall soldier with a black beard and bold black eyes, named Vasco Nuñez de Balboa, told of a better country farther to the west where a great river flowed.

"Why not sail there?" he asked Enciso. "The Indians of that country do not dip their arrows in the poison curare. We can build our town in peace, and grow our food."

19

Everyone agreed that this was wise advice. No time was wasted in leaving the forest of poisoned arrows.

In the new country by the river the Spaniards were able to work in peace at the building of their new town. They felled the biggest trees from the forest and sawed them into boards and beams; they gathered clay from the river's edge and molded it into bricks; and they collected all the stones they could find in the neighborhood. It was a little town which began to rise on the hot soil near the river, but it had a strong fort, and it received a very long name: Santa Maria de la Antigua del Darien. All seemed to go very well until the soldiers grew dissatisfied with Commander Enciso because he forbade them to trade for gold with the friendly Indians. They revolted and chose for their new leader the soldier who had first told them of this new country, Vasco Nuñez de Balboa, as skillful at making friends with the Indians as he was in fighting them. Enciso was sent back to a Spanish port, swearing that he would take his revenge for this revolt.

With the new leader, Pizarro and his soldiers set out to explore the country, to search for the gold treasures they thought were stored in the thatched huts of the Indians. They found only some gold jewelry and carved gods. But one day when they were weighing and melting these, an Indian chief approached them and said: "What is this, Christians? Is it for such a little thing that you destroy the villages on these shores, and banish yourselves from your homeland? If you have so much love for gold, I'll tell you where you may satisfy your greed. Six suns' march away to the south there is a great country where there is more gold than there is water in the sea.

March to the west over the jungle mountains until you come to a great ocean. Then march south for six suns. But along the way, there rule powerful kings, and you must have more soldiers than you have now to conquer them.

"A country where there is more gold than there is water in the sea!" said Balboa, his black eyes sparkling in wonder. "I will conquer it for the King of Spain, and bring knowledge of our God to its people. I will become rich and famous!"

From then on, Balboa and Pizarro and their soldiers could talk of nothing else but the country of gold.

"Of course," Balboa said, "we are not ready to conquer that rich country. But we may at least try to find the ocean the Indian chief talked about. Perhaps it is the great southern sea our Spanish sailors have tried to find for so many years."

At last, one morning, they buckled on their swords, took their crossbows, their spears, and their arquebuses, and with their steel armor as bright as glass in the sun, they entered the deep forest which covered the mountains to the west followed by a long line of Indians carrying cases of food on their backs.

"Think! What a glorious road we are traveling!" cried Balboa, leading his men on.

"Ah, but a hard road, too," thought the soldiers.

Up and up they climbed. It was hot and humid. At almost every step they had to cut their way through the lianas which wound along the ground and up the trees like endless snakes.

In every Indian village through which they passed Balboa was kind and polite to the people and made them his friends. It was only when they came to the country ruled by the cacique Quarega that they met his Indian warriors with feathers

in their hair and white lines painted on their faces—they were ready for war. The arquebuses boomed, the arrows flew; a fierce battle was fought. Many of Balboa's soldiers were wounded, but they put the Indians to flight. And then they went on—up and up the mountains.

Finally, they neared the top of the highest peak and Balboa gave the order to stop. He felt it fitting that only he should first behold the sight on the other side. "Wait," he said. Alone he went to gaze down from the mountain top upon a great sea which spread toward the west. It was indeed the blue southern ocean—later to be known as the Pacific. Balboa called to his soldiers. "Come. Kneel and pray with me," he said. "Our wish, as you see, has been fulfilled. What the Indian chief told us about the sea is true. Surely, what he said about the kingdom where there is as much gold as there is water in the sea must be true also. So let us sing a hymn of praise."

The Spaniards cut some trees to make a cross upon which they engraved the names of the King and Queen of Spain. Then they continued their trip down the mountain side.

When they reached the foot of the mountain, Balboa took eighty men with him to the beach where a solemn ceremony was enacted. He ordered his soldiers to stand at arms while he entered the sea up to his waist and thundered: "This sea with all it contains now belongs to the King of Spain. I will fight anyone who tries to take possession of it."

And, feeling that he had won much glory, Balboa came proudly out of the sea.

Pizarro, standing on the beach with the soldiers felt very proud, too, for he knew that he had taken part in an event of great importance, he was one of the first white men to see the ocean for which so many captains had searched in vain. The ocean which, perhaps, led to China, India, the old countries which Columbus wanted to find.

As Balboa had said, it was not yet time to march south to the Land of Gold. Instead, they visited the shores of the southern sea and some of the islands where Indian divers gave them a little bag full of beautiful pearls. Balboa kept these for his King and his Queen. Now, they must take the way home, Balboa thought, and they climbed over the jungle mountain back to Santa Maria de la Antigua del Darien.

"Some day soon," said Balboa, "I will return to the southern sea to build a port and some ships. And from there I shall sail to the Land of Gold. It will be easier to sail on the sea than to march along the shore."

But Balboa's wish never came true. The King of Spain was very pleased about the discovery of the great sea, and he was delighted with the pearls. He made Balboa an Admiral of the Southern Ocean, but sent a new Governor to Santa Maria. This Governor, to be sure that he would have things his own way, ordered Balboa beheaded. Then on the southern sea he built the port that Balboa had dreamed of. He called it Panama. It was the first city of white men on the great ocean. For a long time after that, neither the Governor nor any other Spaniards continued the search for the Land of Gold. But everyone talked much of it.

For many more years, Pizarro continued to fight the Indians in the countries north and south of Panama, to win more land and more gold for his King, and little for himself.

"I am getting old," he thought, "and I am tired of being a soldier. It has brought me neither fame nor riches." Being a conqueror did not seem to him as wonderful now as it did when he was a little swineherd. Since he had been given some land and some slaves in payment for the long years he served the King of Spain, he decided to build a house and become a planter.

So Captain Pizarro put away his sword and his armor. He thought that he would never again sail away to fight in an unknown land.

The Planters
and the Priest

Often, after a day's work in the fields, tall, proud Pizarro and small, round Diego de Almagro, a soldier friend whom Pizarro had invited to his plantation, would sit under a palm tree to talk of their past adventures. Pizarro, on these occasions, loved to repeat the words of the Indian chief, for he had never forgotten them.

"The country where there is as much gold as there is water in the sea," he would say. "Think of it, Diego—as much gold as there is water in the sea. What a wonderful country that must be. And surely the Indian chief told the truth, for I have heard again about it. It is said that the walls of the Emperor's palaces are of gold, and so are the flowers in his gardens!"

Sometimes their friend Hernando de Luque, the priest, would come trotting up on his mule, for he loved to hear these soldiers' stories. The story of the Land of Gold interested him most of all.

"Well," Hernando said one day, "why don't you, Captain, find out where that country lies? Your arm is still strong enough to carry the sword. And you would still make a more glorious figure in your steel helmet than you do in your straw hat."

"I do not wish to take up my sword again," answered

27

Pizarro. "Why, I am nearly fifty-five years of age. And, besides, I am too poor to buy the ships and hire the soldiers. Some younger captain, perhaps, will go there sometime."

Thus Pizarro and his friends went on talking of the Land of Gold. Like most men who lived in these times, they did not think it a crime to take countries away from their people. Since it was done for their kings and to spread knowledge of the white man's God, they saw no wrong in it.

One evening the priest came galloping, his cassock waving behind, crying: "Did you hear the news, did you hear? An unknown country to the north called Mexico has just been won for our King by a captain named Hernando Cortés. He vanquished the armies of a powerful emperor who ruled in fabulous cities. And he found so much gold that our soldiers use it to weigh down their ships!"

"Hernando Cortés!" said Pizarro as he helped the priest down from his mule. "Why, he is my cousin! He comes from the same part of Spain as I do."

"Your cousin or not, this Cortés is now the most glorious man in all the Spanish lands, in all Europe. Doesn't this give you the desire to sail and find that other country, where there is as much gold as there is water in the sea? What wonderful adventure, and what fame would be yours!"

Pizarro thoughtfully stroked his beard. "It is wiser," he said, "to let a younger and richer man undertake this adventure. Good ships will be needed, for I have heard that the sea is stormy in that part of the world. Many soldiers must be hired, for it is said that the emperor of that land has big armies."

28

"We could sell the plantation," said Almagro, as he looked over the fields of growing corn and yellow wheat.

But Pizarro shook his head. "No, that would not bring enough."

"Listen," said Hernando quietly, "no other captain in all of Spain knows as much about fighting the Indians as Captain Pizarro. And if it is the lack of money which stops you, I know a friend who will help you pay for the ships and the soldiers." The priest smiled. "I see in your black eyes, Captain, that the adventure tempts you. Think of it."

Pizarro thought about it all night, all day, all week.

"By my Toledo sword," he finally said, "I can still fight for my King and for my country. And, really, I am bored on this plantation. I'll sell it, throw away that planter's straw hat, polish my armor and sail away."

Hernando, the priest, as he had promised, found the money which they needed. He also went to the Governor to ask his permission for the hiring of the soldiers. But the old man refused.

"Perhaps," Hernando said to him, "we could make you a partner in our enterprise. Then you would receive your share of the Land of Gold."

"Hm . . . that is different," said the avaricious man. "Would I have to pay something too?"

"Only a little, perhaps. But I think my friends will agree to give you one-fifth of the gold they find."

One-fifth of all the gold! The Governor's eyes were bright with greed. "That pleases me enough," he said. "Well, we will write all that down on a paper, make a contract. And you have my permission to hire the men and to sail."

While the priest was thus doing his part, Pizarro sold his land and his horses and his cows, and Almagro looked for the ships and went around the town calling for soldiers.

He found only two sailing ships; not very big nor very seaworthy. Pizarro gave a worried look at the old planks along their rounded flanks, at their patched-up sails, and at the worn spider web of their riggings. "They will have to do," he muttered as he walked their creaky decks.

As for the soldiers, only one hundred in the town dared to risk their lives in the dangerous journey.

"Why should we be as foolish as you are?" the people of Panama said when they were asked to join in the adventure. "Who would believe in your fairyland of gold except children?" And they laughed.

"Never mind their mockery," said Pizarro. "Some day we will laugh at them. Even with two ships and one hundred soldiers I will conquer the Land of Gold."

It was decided that Pizarro would leave first in the bigger ship, and that Almagro would follow in the other as soon as he had bought all the food, all the arms, and hired some more soldiers.

"So that you can find me," said Pizarro, "I'll notch the trees in all the places where we stop along the way."

The things that Pizarro needed were now carried on board his ship: casks of flour, wine, water, pigs, hens and cows; horses to ride in battle; spears and crossbows, to use against the Indians; and hatchets and glass beads, to win their friendship. When all had been safely put in place, Pizarro climbed

upon his deck and gave the order to raise anchor.

Amidst cries of good wishes from his two friends and the jeers of the crowd gathered on the shore, the Captain sailed away toward the south where, it was said, he would find the Land of Gold.

Hunger
in the Swamps

With its sails rounded like puffs of white clouds, Pizarro's ship sailed on. How far were the cities of the powerful Emperor? Six suns' journey, as the Indian chief had said? At last Pizarro would find out.

[First voyage]

After many days, the Spaniards came to a river and sailed into it through sleepy brown swamps. Far away, at the edge of the swamps, a forest rose threateningly like a fence of grey trunks, roots and lianas woven together with patches of green. Black buzzards, cried down from the highest limbs of dead trees as if to say: "Go away, travelers. This is not a country where men can live. The crocodiles that rest in the swamps will devour you; the poisonous snakes in the forest will put you to death; the mosquitoes and hunger will destroy you. Go away, go away . . ."

They dropped anchor near a clump of twisted trees, chasing the crocodiles away with the noise, and they stepped ashore. It was hot and the ground was muddy. The soldiers marched with difficulty in their stiff steel mail and heavy boots. After trying for a while they decided that there could

33

not be much to explore in this dead country, still less to eat. So they returned to their ship and sailed down the river.

Another place where they anchored, farther south, was no better. There were still the brown swamps and the treacherous forest.

"This is a land such as we see in our nightmares," said Pizarro. "We must turn back to the sea at once."

But there seemed to be no safe place in that country, not even on the water. Blown by the wind, the sea began to swell into high mountains and sink into deep valleys which threatened to swallow the ship. Across the sky, black clouds made the day dark as night.

For ten days the wind blew and howled so fiercely that, when it finally abated, the voyagers were sick from fright and weariness and weak with hunger. Their food was gone.

Could they go on in a battered ship with its sails all torn? Pizarro thought not. And so they turned about to land once more among the swamps.

"Where is the Land of Gold which you promised us?" Pizarro's men cried. "Is it this dreadful country from which even the birds and the wild animals flee for fear of starving? You were a fool to believe in your fairyland, and so were we to trust your promises. And we would be greater fools to die of hunger here. Let us return to Panama."

"Your hearts are as weak as sparrows'," said Pizarro, "Have courage! You will see that at the end you will be well rewarded for your suffering. We shall presently send our ship northward to a Spanish port with half the men to fetch food and find Almagro, while the other half will wait here with me. Then, after we have refreshed ourselves, we shall resume our trip."

So the ship departed. After watching it disappear, far away to the north, the soldiers who remained with Pizarro set about looking for something to eat. All they could find were some sour berries, bitter herbs and the shellfish on the shore.

One week went by. Two weeks, three weeks. . . . When, at the end of six weeks, the ship returned laden with food, twenty soldiers had died of hunger and those who still lived were ragged and dirty.

But men with full stomachs seldom despair. After they had eaten a good meal, the weary soldiers began to think again of the Land of Gold. They were ready to sail on.

"Very well," said Pizarro. "On to the south then, to see what we can find. But first let's give a name to this sad place. Let us call it Port of Hunger."

The two ships set forth again toward the south while all eyes watched the shore for a sign that they were approaching the Land of Gold. But the farther they went, the more threatening the shore looked. The jungle now came to the edge of the sea, and in places the roots of the mangrove trees slipped into the sea like millions of legs, as if the forest was really on its way to invade the ocean.

Smoke that rose suddenly above the trees caused Pizarro to anchor his ships near the shore and send a boat with some armed men to investigate. No town could lie thus in the midst of the jungle, but perhaps it was a village where food could be gathered. The men indeed found a little hamlet of thatched huts, but what they saw in the open space surrounded by the huts sent them running back to their boat, shivering with fear. It was a dead Indian roasting over the fire. They were in the country of the cannibal Caribs!

They set sail quickly and stopped at another village hidden from the sea by the mangrove trees. It seemed such a good place to rest that Pizarro thought they would stay there a while. Since the Indians had fled upon the Spaniards' arrival, Pizarro sent out some scouts to watch the hills and the forest while he entered the village.

But the Indians had left only to spy in safety on the strange men who had landed in their country. They soon came back, all painted with yellow and white lines, and with their head-feathers flying. Yelling their war cries, they fell upon the scouts like flocks of wild cockatoos, filling the air with arrows. Then as suddenly as they had come, they disappeared into the woods, only to come out again near the village to attack Pizarro and his men. Pizarro received them like the valiant Captain that he was, swinging his sword right and left, thus giving heart to his soldiers.

The Indians fought fiercely against the Spanish swords and spears, but they were struck with fear when they saw that their darts and arrows could not pierce the steel helmets and the padded mail. Leaving many dead and wounded on the ground, they ran back into the forest.

The battle was won. But the Spaniards were so exhausted that Pizarro called them to a war council and said: "I think the time has come to make a grave decision. Consider our plight: four of our men are dead; many of us are wounded—I have received seven wounds; our ship is as creaky as an old

cask with rusty staves; and Almagro has not found us. For
these reasons I think it wiser to return north and ask our
Governor to help us with new ships and more soldiers."

The soldiers—some with bandaged heads, others with arms
in slings, some wearily leaning on their spears—all agreed that

it was indeed a wise thing to do. "How can so few of us face the army of the powerful Emperor. Yes, let's go back."

"We must realize, however," continued Pizarro, "that if we were to return to Panama the people there would mock us. Would it not be better to repair our forces in the town of Chicama, which is near Panama, and wait there for Almago?"

The men agreed, and so it was done.

And what of Almagro all this time? He did sail with a shipload of soldiers, as was the order. He followed Pizarro by the notched trees. He sailed past the swamp country; past the cannibal hamlet; past the village of the mangrove trees where he lost an eye in a fight with the Indians. He sailed much farther, until he saw villages and towns of sun-dried clay painted in white among fields of vegetables and corn. Here frightened Indians gave him painted vases, and jewelry, and gods of gold. They told him that they knew about the country of the powerful Emperor.

And just as Pizarro asked, "Where, where is Almagro?" Almagro wondered, "Where is Captain Pizarro? No doubt," he said, "he has not gone farther with his old ship. I must have sailed past him during the night." And he sailed back north until he reached the town of Chicama, where he finally met Pizarro. How happy they were to embrace each other!

The Town on
the River of Emerald

It was decided that Diego de Almagro should go to the Governor in Panama to request more soldiers and ships. Pizarro meanwhile remained in the town of Chicama to repair his health and that of his men.

The Governor, who looked like a cross old crow in his black dress, was not pleased with Almagro's story of their adventures. He struck the arm of his leather chair and said: "You have sailed with two hundred men and two ships, and behold the results! Many soldiers have perished; I am told that those who have returned are mostly ill and that your ships are but fit to be broken up; and what have you found? Only a little gold and some man-eating Caribs. Upon my word, your Land of Gold is but a child's tale."

"It is true that we have found little gold," said Almagro. "However, the Indians we met said that they knew about the rich country."

"No," said the Governor, shaking his head over his ruffled collar. "I do not believe that. Not only do I refuse to help you, but I will never again let our fine Spanish soldiers and our good Spanish ships be lost in your silly adventure."

"Your Excellency has agreed to pay his share of this voyage in return for his share of the gold of that rich country. But you have not given up so much as three pesos, while we have already spent our fortune. If you do not help us now our glorious enterprise will fail. Perhaps you no longer wish to share the burden, as well as the glory, of this adventure. Then pay us your part of what we have spent, for this you owe to us; and leave the affair to my friends and me."

"Enough of your insolence!" said the Governor, raising his head as high as he could. "You should be punished for this. Yes, punished also for murdering our soldiers."

"Your Excellency must pay his part if he wishes to share the fruits of this adventure. You do not even sweat or toil for them."

"I will leave the partnership *only* if you pay me four thousand pesos besides," said the Governor.

"We will be so happy if you let us alone," said Almagro, "that we will agree to forego what you already owe us."

"That is not enough! I said that I wanted four thousand pesos besides!"

"We will pay you three hundred!"

"You must give me two thousand!"

"Five hundred!"

"One thousand!"

"One thousand then!" cried Almagro. "I do not have them, but I shall be delighted to borrow them to be rid of you."

"That will do," said the Governor. "I will record the fact

that I am no longer your partner and give you permission to go on in your adventure."

The Captain went to see his friend, the priest, who was quite cheerful. "Do not worry," he said, "I'll help you buy the ships and hire the soldiers. But as we are only three partners now, we must draw up a new contract. We shall agree that the Land of Gold be divided into three parts. One part for Captain Pizarro, one for you, and one for me. We will divide in the same way any gold, precious stones, and pearls which you may find. Then everything will be in order."

Again, Hernando de Luque kept his promise. Soon, two new ships which Pizarro was to command swayed at anchor in the harbor of Panama. Indians carrying boxes and casks were climbing up the gangplanks like ants along twigs. Then up went Pizarro and Almagro, and after them one hundred and sixty soldiers and sailors—some with crossbows, some with spears, some with arquebuses, some pushing their horses before them.

The people of Panama, of course, watched these preparations with a mocking eye. Pizarro seemed even more crazy to them now than when he departed for his first voyage. Did he not have his fill of the wild jungle during his first trip? On the day of the sailing they came again to the wharf to send him away with their jeers.

But Pizarro was undisturbed by it all. As his ship sailed toward the high sea, and the little town of Panama with its green jungle passed out of sight, he reflected over the stories of the Land of Gold, and his faith in their truth was stronger than ever.

[*Second* Because Pizarro's ships were now guided by an expert *voyage*] pilot named Bartholomew Ruiz, who took advantage of the good wind that was blowing toward the south, they soon reached the villages of white clay which Almagro had seen before.

The Indians there offered them so much gold that it gave Pizarro an idea. "It is plain that we will not feel safe on these shores until we have more soldiers," he said to Almagro. "One of us must sail back to Panama to show this gold. Upon seeing it, men will say, 'Ah, so the story of the Land of Gold is true. Captain Pizarro is not such a fool.' They will be eager to join us. Even the Governor will want them to go."

"Good!" said Almagro. "*I* will go if you wish. With this gold I will also obtain more food and more arms. And perhaps another ship."

"While you are away," said Pizarro, "I will explore the country with my soldiers, and Bartholomew Ruiz will sail in the other ship to see what lands lie to the south." So, Almagro and Ruiz bid goodbye to Pizarro and sailed, one toward the north, the other toward the south. Then Pizarro climbed on his horse and departed with his men into the country. They climbed higher and higher up hills which went almost to the clouds. They descended into deep valleys as dark and dreadful as the inside of a witch's kettle, where serpents, frogs, and salamanders boil in the stew. The serpents were there, as big as tree trunks; so were the frogs, keeping company with the green crocodiles. There were monkeys, who made faces at the soldiers, and parrots shrieking among the leaves.

Sometimes a soldier slipped into a pool of water and was

devoured by a crocodile. Poisonous snakes struck from under fallen trees. And as always there were Indians who shot their arrows from behind the trees.

After some weeks had gone by, the food they had taken along gave out, and hunger, like a monster hovering over the explorers, killed the weakest among them. The wild potatoes and the coconuts which they found on the way were not enough to feed them.

"There is no use searching for the Land of Gold here," decided Pizarro at last. "It is still farther south, no doubt. We must return to the villages on the shore and wait for our ships."

"And *we* will sail back to Panama," grumbled the soldiers. "Let other fools look for your land. All we want is a country where we have a roof over our heads and beds to sleep on, and food on our tables."

They would have revolted when they reached the shore but for Ruiz's timely arrival. The story the pilot had to tell and the two strange Indians he brought with him made them forget their misery.

Never had they seen such beautiful robes as the ones the Indians wore. They were made of wool as fine as silk, dyed in red, purple, yellow and sky-blue, and embroidered with birds, flowers and animals of all colors. And what rich bracelets! What fine necklaces of gold were tied around their arms and necks!

"Ah," said Ruiz, "we saw wonderful things as we sailed south! Towns with wide streets and white houses with thatched roofs! We saw fields of corn and sweet potatoes and plaintain, and orchards of banana trees, and cocoa. The shores

were lined with people wearing cotton dresses of all colors, who watched us sail by, wondering, no doubt, whether we had descended from the sky. There were groves of fine mahogany and ebony trees and scented trees which made the air sweet.

"Then, one day at sea, we sighted a big raft with two masts and a cotton sail approaching us. It was made of wood as light as feathers. It carried vases and drinking vessels of carved gold and silver, and clothes of wool and cotton finer than are to be found in all Spain. These two Indians were passengers on the raft, which they called a balsa. Their city, they say, is larger than those we have seen, and lies far to the south. Its name is

45

Tumbez. And they say that gold and precious stones are as common in the Emperor's palaces as pebbles on the beach.

"After we encountered the balsa we sailed until we crossed the equator. Even if we do not accomplish more, at least I will be proud to have been the first captain to have crossed the line on these seas. And my name will be remembered."

"All these things," said Pizarro, "are wonderful to hear. You have done well, Bartholomew Ruiz. It may be that the country of these Indians is the Land of Gold. We must sail and see."

Tired and sick as they were, the soldiers wanted to sail at once; but they had to wait for Almagro.

He was not long in arriving with more good news.

"We guessed well," he said to Pizarro after they embraced each other. "The people were filled with wonder at the gold I brought back to Panama. Eighty soldiers begged to join us and they are here with us, as you can see. I have also brought food and all the things we need. There is a new Governor in Panama; he wished us much success."

"All is well then," said Pizarro. "Perhaps we are at the end of our trials. Let us resume our journey."

The travelers went back to sea, but soon found themselves in the midst of a tempest. The thunder, the wind, and the waves, like three furious madmen trying to outshout each other, joined in a dreadful chorus. Even though the storm lasted seven days, their ships withstood the ordeal.

Then the wind ceased and all the clouds were swept from the sky.

Sailing close to the shore, the explorers soon sighted the

country described by Ruiz, where the Indians were busy ploughing their fields and where the trees were laden with beautiful fruit. And presently they came to a stop near a town of white houses with golden roofs of dried palm leaves. After giving the order to drop anchor, Pizarro climbed upon the deck under the flapping sail to have a better look. The arrival of his ships had interrupted the Indians in their occupations: women in long striped robes carrying water jars on their heads, or babies in their arms; men with bundles of fruit or jars of wine on their backs, or still holding the tools of their trades—all were running toward the shore in great excitement. Pizarro admired the green hills which rose behind the town, one upon another, until they reached the blue mountains whose summits were hidden high in the clouds.

"This town is Tacamez," said one of the Indians aboard. "And the river which you see there behind it is called the River of Emerald, because of all the precious stones that are found on its shores."

Suddenly a sailor perched on a shroud shouted, "I see armed warriors lining the shore. Thousands of them!"

"I do not like that," said Pizarro with a bitter smile. "These people must be very civilized indeed, for they have not only good houses and streets and cultivated fields, but armies as well."

"And look at those canoes filled with soldiers," said Almagro. "They come to fight us!"

"We shall try to land with some horses, nevertheless," ordered Pizarro. "They have never seen horses. Nay, they have never even seen a man riding an animal. They will think that our cavaliers are terrible monsters, and that will frighten them. I have seen this sight put many a brave Indian warrior to flight in the north."

He and thirty cavalrymen bucked on their armor and their swords, and, with their horses, were landed on the beach. But what was wrong? The Indians showed not a trace of fear!

Bristling with spears, their lines advanced like giant porcupines, closer and closer, all around the horsemen. Thousands against thirty.

Suddenly a horse reared and threw its rider to the ground. What a marvelous and terrible thing! A two-headed creature that can cut himself into two different beings, one on four legs, the other on two. The Indians stopped, amazed. Some of them even dropped their spears and ran into the town. This was the opportune moment for the Spaniards. They turned and galloped back toward the ships. They were saved.

Pizarro ordered the anchors raised at once, and the ships sailed out to sea.

"I think that we are deceiving ourselves," said Almagro as the pilots steered toward the north. "Never shall we conquer this country with one hundred soldiers. We must have ten times as many. I propose to return to Panama. When the Governor sees the two Indians with the embroidered robes, and hears about the wonderful things we have seen we should easily be able to recruit enough infantrymen and cavalrymen to fill several ships. In the meantime, Captain Pizarro, perhaps you can wait for me in a safe place. If we all go back, the Governor will say that we have failed and never again will he permit us to sail south."

"I will have none of your plan," said Pizarro gruffly. "It is all very well for you. But you do not know what it is to remain and face starvation in the swamps or in the wild forest. You would not choose that for yourself!"

"That is an insult," cried Almagro. "I am not less courageous than you, and if you fear the jungle, then sail to Panama yourself and *I* will remain here."

Both captains put their hands to their swords. They would have fought had not their friends made them see their folly. After talking more reasonably, they decided that it would be best for Almagro to sail to Panama, and for Pizarro to wait in some safe place.

But where was this safe place to be found, they wondered, as they sailed north. Not in that country, to be sure. The alarm had been sounded in all the Indian villages on the shores. Whenever the two ships dropped their anchors, Indian warriors, with their darts, and their bows and arrows, stood ready to drive the Spaniards into the sea.

"See the difficult choice we must make," said Pizarro. "If we land here the Indians will kill us, and if we land farther to the north we will starve to death in the swamps and the wild forest."

"I have it!" said Almagro, pointing toward the prow of the ship. "On our way here we passed a small island not far to the north. It is scarcely larger than a rock and few trees grow there but it will be a safe harbor for your ship."

"I remember," said Pizarro. "It is a lonely place, but there we will be safe from the Indians. Let us go."

What shouts of anger were heard when the voyagers arrived at the tiny island and Pizarro told the men of his own ship that they would remain there with him while Almagro's ship went north.

"Ah, indeed, what choice is there for us. To die on this rock, to die fighting the Indians, or to die in the forest! We have had enough of this voyage. In hunting for your Land of Gold we are chasing a shadow: the farther we go, the farther away that land is. And what of the gold we have found? Did we share in it? Oh, no! It is used to lure others into this adventure. All the treasures we can show for our hardships are cross-bows and arrows!"

So desperate were the men that they gave letters to their friends on Almagro's ship begging that they be delivered to relatives in Panama. These letters told of their misery and asked the Governor to send a ship to rescue them.

Almagro learned about the letters and knew that the Governor must never see them. If he did, he would refuse Almagro new ships. The ship was searched from holds to decks and the letters hurled into the sea. All but one. That one letter had been hidden by a sailor in a ball of cotton which Pizarro was sending as a gift to the Governor's wife. Almagro never thought of looking there.

The Governor's lady was pleased when she received the gift. But her eyes filled with tears when she read the letter that fell out of the cotton. The letter told of the sufferings of the soldiers, how they were left to starve on a barren island, and implored the Governor to send a ship to bring them home. It ended thus:

> Look out, Señor Governor,
> For the drover when he's near,
> Since he goes home to get the sheep
> For the butcher who stays here.

The poor lady showed her husband the sad message. In a fit of anger, he called for Almagro.

"So this is what you have been doing these past months! You leave our King's soldiers to perish on that barren rock while you come here to lure more of them into that mad voyage."

"We will fail in that voyage only if you do not give us more men to help us," answered Almagro. "You have seen the two Indians with the beautiful robes. They have told us things which make us believe that we will surely find the Land of Gold!"

"Indeed! *You* believe . . . And because you believe, you ask me to let you sacrifice our soldiers! *I* believe that your Golden Land is but an idle dream. Two Indians in embroidered robes are hardly enough to convince me!"

"But we have shown you the carved gods of gold, the fine gold vases, the necklaces, the rings, and many other things. . ."

"Gold trinkets were found near Panama too, but there was no powerful kingdom for all that."

"Yes, but we have seen beautiful cities, with wide streets, with orchards as fine as we see in Spain. . ."

"I do not want to be bothered any longer with your fantastic stories! Never again will I permit you to sail from Panama. Furthermore, I will send a ship at once to rescue those poor wretched soldiers from the rock in the middle of the sea." Almagro was hastily dismissed.

While Almagro was thus pleading in vain for help, Pizarro waited. He was forlorn and hungry; and as he caught the resentful glances of his men and heard their angry mutterings, he knew that there would soon be rebellion if he did not act to prevent it. So he did a very desperate thing; he ordered aboard the ship the most discontented men and sent them away to Panama, keeping with him only those who were entirely devoted.

"It is better," he thought, "to be with fewer but safer comrades."

But, when the ship was gone, they were without shelter from the unceasing rain. Their wet clothes clung limply to their bodies. When hunger began to strike them down, even the faithful thought only of going home, of leaving Pizarro to search alone for the Land of Gold.

Weeks went by. The men grew so feeble from hunger and exposure that they were barely able to crawl on their hands and knees in search of shellfish left by the tides. They were even too weak to shout for joy when, at last, they sighted sails on the horizon and the Governor's ships dropped anchor off the rock. Only Pizarro had enough strength to greet the captain of the rescue ships when he stepped ashore followed by some sailors carrying baskets of food.

"When you and your men have partaken of this food, Captain Pizarro," said the Governor's messenger, "you will come on board with us, for it is the Governor's order that no one be left on this bare island. Your search for the Land of Gold has come to a sorry end."

Pizarro's black eyes flashed as he answered, "I will die rather than leave this island and give up the search."

"These are the Governor's orders," said the Captain, "and I must execute them. But here," he added, "I have a letter for you."

It was a letter from Almagro and Hernando de Luque. Pizarro read it while his men, like famished animals, gobbled up the food.

"Do not return on the Governor's ships," the letter said. "To do so would be to give up forever our chances to find the Land of Gold. Stay on the island and we will try to send you the ships that will take you south once more. Hope and courage!"

Hope and courage. Yes, he must keep up both. Starved and ragged, he lifted his head with determination, and called to his men who were already preparing to embark.

"Go if you wish," he cried. "As for me, I will stay on this rock. Alone if I must." Then he drew his sword and traced a

line on the sand from east to west, and said: "My friends and comrades, on the south side of this line are toil, hunger, naked-ness, the drenching storm—and even death. But there also lies the Land of Gold with its treasures. On the north side are ease and pleasure; the Governor's ships to take you back to Panama, and poverty. Choose what befits a Spaniard. For my part, I go south!" And he stepped over the line.

The soldiers looked at him for a while, not knowing what to do. Then Bartholomew Ruiz, the pilot, walked to the line and crossed to Pizarro's side. One by one, twelve more crossed the line and stood by Pizarro, even though they knew that death instead of riches might be their reward.

"Very well," said the Captain of the Governor's ships. "You can stay to starve on your rock if you choose. But even if you escape death, you shall not escape the Governor's wrath."

"In doing so we follow our own consciences," answered Pizarro. "We will only ask you to take Bartholomew Ruiz on your ship. He knows much about ships, and will help Diego de Almagro and Father Hernando de Luque to fit some new ones, if they obtain the Governor's permission."

After the ships were gone, Pizarro and his comrades gathered to make plans.

"I think," said Pizarro, "that it would be folly to stay on this barren island. The Captain of the Governor's ships has left us food enough for only a few weeks, while our friends might not come to our rescue for many months."

"That is true," said one of the soldiers. "But how shall we leave?"

"And where shall we go?" asked another.

"There is another island to the north," said Pizarro. "It may be better than our rock. If we build a raft with the old casks left by our ships we may sail there to explore it."

His companions were so anxious to leave their island that they set to work at once gathering the old casks and tying them together with rags which they twisted into ropes. It made a clumsy raft but a very seaworthy one. They loaded it with their few cases of food, and pushed it into the surf.

By rowing, each man in his turn, and with the help of a small sail fashioned out of their own clothes, they reached the new island in three days.

They found it much better than the rock. There were woods and some meadowland where hares and pheasants hid in the grass. And there was a stream of fresh water. They built huts to protect themselves from the rain that clattered ceaselessly on the leaves; with their crossbows they hunted the hares and pheasants, and from the stream they took their drinking water. At least they were no longer hungry.

Each morning and night, Pizarro said the prayers, and all day they looked to the north for the welcome sight of a sail. Months passed. But they saw only the waves that curled white at the top, the sea birds that came and went and sometimes, the fins of a shark, or a whale that hurried by.

At the end of the seventh month, a small white sail suddenly appeared, growing and growing, and swinging, far away. It was a Spanish ship! Pizarro's comrades danced and shouted on the beach, but the captain strained his eyes to see whether other ships were coming, farther away.

"Only one," he sighed at last. "The Governor was not generous."

Bartholomew Ruiz was in command.

"Ah," said the brave pilot as he stepped ashore. "It wasn't easy to get even that lone ship. Father de Luque and Diego de Almagro visited the Governor every day for many weeks; but he would not listen to their pleas. At last, Father de Luque told him that you undertook this voyage for the glory of our King and of Spain and that he would risk punishment if he refused to help. He must have been frightened by that for he said, "Very well, I will let you have one ship, with the necessary food and arms. Not more. And I command Captain Pizarro to be back in Panama in six months, even if he finds nothing. That is my order.""

"And here I am, Captain, with not many men, but with wishes of success from your friends."

"Thank you for what you have done, Bartholomew Ruiz," said Pizarro. "Now let's count how many we are. . . . Twenty-eight. Twenty-eight to conquer the armies of the powerful Emperor when we find them! But we shall do our best. Let us sail to the city of Tumbez. The alarm along the shore may not have traveled as far as that country. We shall see. And we shall find whether or not it is the Land of Gold. . ."

The Flowers of Gold

The wind was contrary, but it blew so gent-
ly, just rounding out the sails, that the ship
plodded on steadily, day after day, toward
[*Third voyage*]   the south.

From his deck, Pizarro saw again the River of Emerald.
They had now crossed the equator. This was as far as they
had gone before, but now they went on along an unknown
country of desert plains, of green valleys speckled with white
cottages, with the snowy mountains far away rising above the
clouds.

After more than three weeks of sailing, they arrived at a
large town where big stone mansions stood among small houses
of white clay like great lords among their humble subjects, and
where balsas sailed to and fro along the shore.

"It is Tumbez," said one of the two Indians on board.

While the Spaniards beheld the town from the railings and
the rigging of the ship, the Indians in their cotton dresses gazed
at them from the shore. They were like a long fringe dyed in
brilliant colors strung along the water's edge.

Slowly six balsas surrounded the ship. They were filled with
soldiers armed with lances and clubs. Pizarro knew that he

must make friends with them, for they outnumbered his men. He called to the warriors and invited to his ship those among them who wore coats of embroidered wool; they were the chiefs. The others, the simple soldiers, wore coats of cotton quilt and bright helmets also of cotton.

The Indian chiefs with smooth brown skins were puzzled by Pizarro's big "balsa" planted with masts all hung with ropes, like trees with vines, where there climbed, not monkeys, but men with white skin, and hair on their chins. They opened their eyes wide as Pizarro showed them up and down the ship, and they went back to their soldiers almost without a word, so great was their surprise.

Soon other balsas, laden with bananas, sweet potatoes, corn, plantain, vegetables, meat and fish for the stranger, came to the ship; and one even carried an animal which made the Spaniards laugh, for they had never seen one like it and, when a sailor pulled its wool, it spat.

"What a strange beast," said one of the soldiers. "A sheep that looks like a camel."

"You are wrong," said another. "It's a camel that looks like a sheep. It's a spitting camel."

"We call it a llama," said their Indian companions. "We make our beautiful embroidered clothes from its wool; we eat its flesh; and it carries our heavy loads across the highest mountains."

After the warriors, the fruit, and the llama, there came on board an Indian who was, no doubt, an important man, perhaps a prince, for everyone showed him great respect. He wore a woolen robe finer and more beautifully embroidered than

the others. Heavy gold jewels hung from his ears. Captain Pizarro welcomed him and took him all over his ship; down the black hold where the food casks were kept; to the place where the chickens, the pigs, the cows were cared for; to the dark room where the voyagers slept; to the shop where the carpenter worked to keep the ship in good repair. He saw and admired everything.

"But, tell me," he asked when he had finished (his countrymen who spoke Spanish repeated his words to Pizarro), "whence come these men so unlike us, dressed not only in wool but in a stuff harder than gold and silver—and more precious perhaps?"

"We have come from a country on the other side of the world," said Pizarro, "where rules the most powerful and noblest king on earth. His armies are all clothed in steel and they are more numerous than the trees in your forests."

"And why have you left that country and come to mine in your tall balsa?"

"Ah," said Pizarro, "my king in time may rule over the whole world, and I have come to tell your people about him. I want also to deliver you from the gods you worship. For you must know that it is only by worshipping our God that you will save your souls!"

The Indian lord remained silent. Perhaps he thought that the bearded chief was ill in his mind. Nevertheless, when he left, he graciously accepted a gift from Pizarro. It was an axe of steel, the metal he admired more than the Spaniards loved gold.

"Now," said Pizarro to his men, "we must astonish these

people. By showing them all the things we have that they have never seen we will make them admire and fear us."

So the next day he sent ashore, with the Indians who spoke Spanish, a bearded soldier, a Negro sailor, a hen, a rooster, and a pig.

From all over the town, the Indians came to see and touch these wonderful things. The ladies admired the soldier's great size and they pulled his beard, and they washed the Negro's face to see if the black would come off. The rooster pleased the Indians very much too. When he began to crow they laughed and clapped their hands.

"What does this creature say?" they wanted to know.

"He greets you and he says that he likes your country," answered the soldier. "Now, my captain wants to give him, the hen, and the pig, to your Governor. Can you tell me where he lives?"

"The *curaca*?" said the Indians. "Come." They led the two men to a large stone house guarded by Indian warriors. It was dark inside, for it had only two windows. This was the *curaca's* mansion.

The prince was so enchanted with his presents that he asked the soldier and the Negro sailor to share some llama meat, potatoes and fruit with him. The meal was served in gold dishes which the soldier liked as much as the food.

Afterwards, the Spaniard and the Negro were taken for a pleasant walk through the town whose houses were made of bricks baked in the sun. They were all but one story high and without windows. The soldier gasped in amazement when he was shown the big fortress filled with soldiers. Its thick walls,

also one story high, were built with stones so well cut that, although they were uncemented, one could not have wedged a piece of paper between them. Then there was the temple. It was low like the houses, and windowless, but so decorated with gold and silver and precious stones, that the soldier could not tear himself away from it.

"Ah," he shouted when he got back to the ship, "there is no doubt that this *is* the Land of Gold . . . but it is also the land of the powerful Emperor," he added, thinking of the big fortress. And he told Pizarro the story of his adventures.

"Yes, it really seems as if at last we have come to the end of our long search," said Pizarro. "Can it be true? I dare not believe it. Tomorrow I shall send another man to look and tell me what he has seen."

The next morning, Pedro de Candia, the cavalier, stepped ashore gloriously attired in his polished steel helmet and armor, with his arquebus on his shoulder, and sword by his side. Again the Indians crowded to the seashore to see the new wonder whose armor gleamed so brightly in the sun.

"Our countrymen who have come with you have told us about the thunder which you carry on your shoulder," Pedro was told. "Will it roar today?"

"It will at your wish," said Pedro. "Do you see that board which leans against the wall? . . . Then watch and hear . . . my thunder looks at the board and. . ."

Boom! At the noise and flash the Indians fell to the ground and hardly dared to look up. The board was shattered.

"You have nothing to fear from the thunder," said Pedro with a broad smile. "It is friendly today. Come now. I want to see the town." And the cavalier walked off amidst the crowd of Indians. He, too, was shown the fortress and the temple—he saw so many things that when he returned to his comrades he did not know where to begin his story.

"This is truly the Land of Gold!" he cried. "Yes, we have found it. The fortress has three walls each as broad as our ship. And the temple! It is a temple to the sun, for the Indians believe that the sun is the god of all. I saw the image of the sun god with rays of light carved in gold. There are carved animals and birds and flowers, all of gold, silver, and precious stones. They make a tapestry on the walls. And I saw the convent of the Virgins of the Sun where beautiful girls live. And now hear! In the garden of the convent there are rows upon rows of flowers and vegetables made of gold! And I saw the work-shops where craftsmen make these beautiful things. I was told about the Emperor. He lives in his palaces up in the mountains, surrounded by armies bigger than those of our King. We are indeed at the end of our hardships. This is the Land of Gold!"

"I doubt no longer," said Pizarro. "This country may be

like a land of fairy tales, but it is real. The Indian chief did not lie to Balboa."

The Captain and his comrades were so joyous that they embraced each other and danced on the decks, and then fell to their knees to give prayers of thanksgiving.

But Pizarro wanted to see more of the country. Tumbez was only one town, after all. What would the others be like? He ordered his men to weigh anchor, and the good pilot Ruiz guided the ship again toward the south.

Many times the travelers brought in their sails near towns with palaces built of stones and windowless houses roofed with straw.

Often balsas came to greet them with gifts of fruit, vegetables and meats. These Indians were good farmers. As his ship glided south, Pizarro saw them in their fields, ploughing with wooden sticks, harvesting, caring for their trees, watching over their llamas, or repairing the canals and aqueducts which brought water from the distant mountains.

And Pizarro was at once happy and worried: happy because he had no doubts about having found the Land of Gold; worried because he could not conquer it with but twenty-eight men. Nay, not even with a thousand. Like all the French, Portuguese, Dutch and English captains who roamed the seas in their frail sailing ships, he had only one thought now. "How can I best conquer, for my King and for my country, this land which I have just discovered?"

He talked this over with his comrades.

"Haven't we seen enough now?" they said. "What could we gain by sailing farther south along these unknown shores?

With our lone ship we would run into dangers we could not overcome. Let us go home and recount our adventures and see about getting ready an army. A big one we shall need if we are to win this country for Spain!"

"Very well," answered Pizarro after thinking a while. "We have won glory enough by discovering a new country and sailing where no white man's ship has ever gone before. Yes, it is time to go back."

Never did the helmsman obey his order with a more joyous heart; never did the sailors climb the rigging with more agility. The ship, its sails flapping, turned toward the north, and, with a good wind at the stern, was on its way back to Panama.

71

The King of Spain
is Pleased

The Governor of Panama was awakened one morning by cries in the street below his window. Through the din he heard these words:

"Captain Pizarro's ship is coming in! Captain Pizarro is back . . ."

"Pizarro?" wondered the Governor going to the window. "Never did I expect to see him again."

Between the palm trees that lined the street, he could see a crowd running past his house toward the harbor, yelling: "Come and see Pizarro's ship! She's back from the south . . ."

"Pizarro!" repeated the Governor. "Has he found and conquered his land of wonder or does he come again for more men and more ships?"

Presently the Governor saw some people running back from the harbor, shouting the news for all to hear: "Pizarro is back . . . Pizarro has found the Land of Gold . . ."

The story of the Land of Gold, of the garden with the flowers of gold, of the temple with the golden walls, of the wonders Pizarro and his men had seen, was soon told all over Panama. It was wonderful news indeed, for everyone thought that Pizarro and his companions had perished in the sea, or had been killed by the savage Indians, or devoured by wild beasts. And now he was back with news of the Land of Gold!

But the Governor was not pleased to hear this.

"Pizarro has found the Land of Gold, but it seems that he has not conquered it. So, of course, he wants more men, more ships, and many other things. But I shall give him nothing. I shall forbid him to sail away. This time nothing will change my mind."

He repeated that to Pizarro the next day when the Captain came to tell his story and ask for help.

"No," the Governor said. "No. I do not wish to help you build a state at the expense of Panama. I do not wish to see more men killed for a few gold toys and some Indian sheep. I will hear no more about the Land of Gold."

Pizarro was broken-hearted. Was his adventure to end now, just when, he thought, the Land of Gold was to be his? He went to Father Hernando de Luque and Almagro, and together they held a council.

"If we cannot find help or get permission to sail south again," said Almagro, "surely a more fortunate captain will come and conquer the land we have discovered."

"Indeed, that's what I fear," said Pizarro. "But what can we do?"

"There is something we can do," said Father Hernando. "I think we should see the King of Spain. After all, it is for Spain and our King that the Land of Gold will be conquered! The King should want to help us, or at least permit us to go on with our adventure."

"That may be very well," said Almagro. "But who will go to the King? Not I. No one will ever make a gnarled old, one-eyed soldier like me wear velvet and silk clothes and a ruffled lace collar."

"And not I," said Pizarro. "I would rather be among the man-eating Indians and the jaguars of the jungle than among the King's courtiers."

"Do not ask me to go," said Father Hernando. "My duties demand that I stay here in Panama. I cannot leave. However, I know a gentleman who is about to sail for our motherland, and we might ask him to see the King."

"It is not wise to entrust our affairs to a stranger," said Almagro. "Captain Pizarro, it seems to me, is the best man for this task. He is a fine-looking soldier and a king may well be pleased with his discourse. Even though he cannot read, he talks like a gentleman."

"Ah," said Pizarro, "again, your wish is that the most unpleasant share befall me. If it is not to starve on a desert island, then it is to face the King and his court!"

"Almagro is right," said Father Hernando. "Only you can tell well the story of your own adventures, sufferings, and discoveries. You must go."

Finally, Pizarro said that he would go.

"Very well, then," said Father Hernando. "Now we must see about buying all the things you need for the voyage. For you must face the King dressed like a prince, not like a poor adventurer."

75

"You must take with you the Indians with the embroidered robes, to whom we have taught Spanish," said Almagro. "You should also bring to the King some of the Indian sheep with the long necks, and some gold vases and carved gods, as well as some beautiful Indian clothes embroidered with animals and flowers. The King will not doubt your story if he sees such evidence of your success."

"That is how Admiral Columbus won the King's favor when he returned from his great voyage," said Father Hernando. "Well, that is good. And now, my children," added the priest softly, "let us hope that you will remain loyal friends, and that you, Captain Pizarro, will never make a decision without consulting us."

It was then decided that Pedro de Candia, Pizarro's comrade, should go with him to help him during the trip.

The three friends parted to make the necessary preparations. Enough money was borrowed to buy Pizarro the finest clothes in Panama, and to pay for the trip.

When all was ready, Pizarro and Pedro climbed on their horses. Followed by the Indians and the llamas bearing the gifts for the King, they departed for the Atlantic side of the Isthmus

of Panama whence ships sailed for Spain.

The little ship that carried Pizarro and his companions ploughed swiftly across the broad ocean and in less than a month came to anchor in the port of Seville.

Pizarro was returning to his motherland, not as the poor simple soldier he was when he left, but as the discoverer of a new country. He was greeted as such by the people of Seville who had already heard the wonderful story of the Land of Gold.

Ah, but what misfortune awaited him! One day, unexpectedly, he encountered Enciso, the former Commander of the *Santa Maria* who had sworn that he would take revenge on the men who had once chased him from his ship. He publicly accused Pizarro of being one of the soldiers who had revolted, and the Captain was presently led into jail!

Pizarro paced the floor of his cell like a caged lion and talked of thrusting his sword through Enciso. Fortunately, the story of the discovery had come to the King's ears, and he was furious when he learned where Captain Pizarro was.

"It is nonsense to jail a captain who comes to lay at my feet a kingdom full of the very gold I need to fight my enemies in

Europe!" the King cried. "I would like to imprison that wicked Enciso himself. Release Captain Pizarro at once and tell him to come to Toledo in haste," commanded the King.

So Pizarro and Candia on horseback, the Indians on foot, and the llamas carrying the gifts for the King, took the long, dusty road to Toledo.

The King was so impatient to hear about the rich kingdom that he could not wait for the weary travelers to rest upon their arrival in Toledo. He ordered them to come before him at once.

"What beautiful gifts you bring me," cried the King as they were laid before him.

He admired the Indians too, and the llamas with their wooly coats from which the fine clothes were made.

Pizarro now told him his long story; of hunger and death in the forest and in the swamps; the storms at sea; the cannibal Indians and the poisoned arrows. The King listened attentively. Tears came to his eyes when Pizarro told the story of the desert rock where thirteen companions had crossed the line traced on the sand. He exclaimed with admiration when he heard about the fine cultivated fields of the new country, the orchards, the pastures full of llamas, the gardens with the flowers of gold and the temple with the golden walls.

"You think, Captain Pizarro, that the Emperor of the country is very powerful?" asked the King finally.

"They say that he is second only to Your Majesty," said Pizarro. "It is said that he has even more soldiers than we have in Spain."

"Do you think two hundred and fifty Spaniards in your

army will be sufficient, Captain?"

"That should do, Your Majesty."

"Very well, Francisco Pizarro," said the King. "You will be rewarded for your courage, and I will tell the Queen and my government to help you, so that you can successfully complete what you have undertaken. I must be off now to join my armies which await me in Italy, Germany, and France."

After the King hurried away from Spain, the Queen ordered his lawyer to draw up an agreement between Pizarro and the government. Pizarro signed the paper with a cross when he had made certain that what it contained was fair to him. Then the Queen's men countersigned it.

No one reading that document would have dared to say that Pizarro was not a great captain. To begin with, he was now allowed to wear the cape bearing the cross of St. Iago, to hang by his side the sword of the hidalgo, and to paint on his escutcheon the black eagle, the two pillars of the King's arms, an Indian city, a ship on the sea, and a llama. He was no longer simply Francisco Pizarro. He was Governor, Captain-General, Adelantado Alguacil-Mayor of the new country now called New Castile by order of the King. Furthermore, no one but Pizarro had the King's permission to conquer it.

Francisco Pizarro was now a great captain.

In return for these honors Pizarro was required to raise an army of two hundred and fifty soldiers, complete with spears, swords, crossbows or arquebuses, armor and horses. He must also get ships to carry them and the food to feed them. Upon setting out from Panama to conquer the Land of Gold he must take priests with him to teach the Indians the Christian faith, treasurers to count the King's share of all the gold found; but no lawyers, for they bred only dispute wherever they went.

And finally he must set out to conquer the country for Spain and for the King, not later than one year after signing the agreement.

In the contract there were provisions made for Pizarro's friends: Almagro was to be Commander of the fortress of Tumbez; and he too was now a hidalgo. Father de Luques was to be Bishop of Tumbez. Bartholomew Ruiz was Grand Pilot of the Southern Ocean. Pedro de Candia was General of the Artillery, and the old comrades of Pizarro who had crossed the line in the sand were made hidalgos.

When this was arranged, Pizarro put on his mantle with the cross of St. Iago, hung his new sword by his side, and with the air of a great nobleman went to visit Trujillo where he had once guarded pigs and dreamed of adventures.

How proud were the people of Trujillo when they beheld their countryman who had become such a famous captain! And how silent with admiration they stood when he told again his tales of the Land of Gold! But proudest of all were Pizarro's brothers who were still living in Trujillo; Hernando, the haughty, cruel, hidalgo; the fearless Gonzales; the younger Juan and Martin. Of course, all four wanted to join their brother in his adventures.

But Pizarro had not gone to Trujillo only to show his coat, his sword and his airs. He wanted soldiers for his conquest. Alas, his countrymen were frightened as much as captivated by his tales. Beside Pizarro's brothers, only a few cared to risk their lives on the other side of the world. And these were so

81

poor that they could not afford to buy a horse, armor, or arms.
Nor could Pizarro, for the King had given him no money. He
was much perplexed until his cousin, Hernando Cortés, the
Conqueror of Mexico came to help him!

"You are learning that the ways of the King are strange," Cortés told Pizarro. "We both have reason to complain. I have given Mexico to the King and now he will forget me. He wishes that you give him this Land of Gold, but he will not give you his soldiers. However, let the Conqueror of the North help the Conqueror of the South. I will give you the money you need."

Pizarro gladly accepted his cousin's help. Thanks to Cortés, he could now put together his little army. He soon enlisted enough men, and acquired three ships which of course, he would have to leave on the Atlantic side of the Isthmus of Panama in exchange for three new ones in which to sail the Southern Ocean. Since there was nothing more for him to do in Spain, he made ready his ships and bade goodbye to his motherland, hoping that if he ever returned it would be as a true conqueror. After a swift voyage he arrived in America.

Pizarro's friends, Diego Almagro and Father Hernando de Luque, were not satisfied by the news he brought from Spain. In the first place, they could not understand why the four brothers spoke as if *they* were Pizarro's old partners. And who was this tall Hernando Pizarro, to look down upon everyone, particularly upon the little Almagro? And why had Pizarro kept for himself all the titles that the Queen had put in the capitulation?

"Is it thus," cried Almagro, "that you treat friends who shared with you in the dangers and the cost of the enterprise when you know your obligation to care for our affairs as well as for your own?"

Said Pizarro: "The country to the south is large enough

for both of us and I promise that you will have your share."

"These are only empty words," exclaimed Almagro. "According to the Queen's agreement, you have everything. I thought that *I* was to be Adelantado, but you have kept that for yourself. You are Captain-General, Governor, and I am but your lieutenant."

"Always," answered Pizarro.

Father Hernando saw that if he did not make peace between his friends it would be bad for all of them; the more so because Almagro said that he would buy ships and conquer New Castile for himself. After much talking, Pizarro consented to let Almagro be Adelantado and Governor of half the country. Although the two men shook hands, Almagro never again trusted Pizarro, and even less his four troublesome brothers.

They were again faced with the problem of finding more soldiers, for many who had come with Pizarro from Spain had deserted upon arriving in the New World when they heard of the poisoned arrows, the fever and starvation, the cannibal Indians and wild beasts they would encounter. But the people of Panama, who knew of these dangers, would not go with Pizarro. At last, tired of trying to gather more men, the old captain decided to leave for the south with a small army.

"I have but one hundred and eighty soldiers and twenty-seven horses," he said. "Not many more than I had before. But the year's time allowed by the Queen for my preparations is about over, and I must go."

And so it was that Pizarro set sail for the conquest of the country whose Emperor had as many soldiers as there are pebbles on a beach.

The Four Corners
of the World

The Indians in the town near the River of
Emeralds beheld one morning a sight that
filled them with dismay. There, upon the
[*The conquest*] sea, the ships of the bearded men were rock-
ing, slowly preparing to anchor! And worse, at the edge of the
forest, the bearded soldiers who had disembarked many days
before to follow their ships along the shore, were coming,
marching on their town!

Although the strangers on their first trip had come as friends,
the Indians had been glad to see them leave. They feared that
the worst would befall them should the big sailing ships ever
come back.

Indeed, this time the greedy men who looked for gold made
no pretensions of being friends. Clad in steel, astride fierce
animals, brandishing sharp swords and sticks that threw light-
ning, they presently fell upon the town like a torrent of fire
from a volcano.

The Indians were too terrified to fight. Men, women, children, old people, all ran out of the town to hide in the woods,
leaving their thatched houses in the hands of their enemies.
The Spaniards wasted no time in pursuit. They wanted only
to search the houses for gold. They found enough vases and

85

emeralds and gold jewelry to make a stack as high as a horse.

After the custom of the Spanish conquerors, Pizarro put aside one-fifth of the loot for the King and divided the rest among his men.

Then he said to them: "The only way to raise an army large enough to fight the Emperor's forces is to send this treasure in the three ships, to be kept for you in Panama, as we have done in the past. At the sight of it, men's greed will be stronger than their fear, and they will join us. In the meantime, we shall march toward the wonderful town of Tumbez."

This was not to the liking of the soldiers who much preferred a voyage in ships to a march over unknown land where the armies of the Emperor might attack them. But the courage and the determination of Pizarro gave them inspiration, and they followed him across the sandy plains that lay ahead of them. They plodded on day after day, and great was their suffering. The sun baked the sand until it burned like clay in an oven and the wind blew it into their eyes. Their feet and those of the horses sank in it under the weight of their heavy armor. They could not find rest even at night, for the breezes which refreshed them also brought mosquitoes to sting them out of their sleep and spread a disease that killed many of them.

But Pizarro would not stop. He hid his own suffering, smil-

ing to those who groaned, helping those who were too tired, caring for those who were sick. Yet, in spite of his courage, his companions would have refused to go on had it not been for the marvelous treasures of Tumbez which soon would be theirs. Or so they thought.

But more misadventures awaited them. On a small island near Tumbez, where Pizarro had repaired with Indian balsas to rest his men, Indian warriors, like wasps swarming out of their nest, sprang out of the woods to attack them in great number. The Spaniards ran for their arms and were instantly ready to stop the Indians with the thrusts of their long pikes, to terrify them with the fire and din of their arquebuses, and to put them to flight with cavalry charges.

It was a complete victory, but at great cost.

When all was still on the field, four Spaniards lay dead, and so many wounded were limping back to camp or crying for help that Pizarro became doubtful. Not with a lame army of a hundred and fifty men—all that remained—could he conquer the Land of Gold. Even the Indian warriors who had just fled would surely try to attack them at night; and they would soon learn to be unafraid of the horses, the arquebuses, and the Spaniards' armor.

Pizarro turned over these dark thoughts in his mind for many days and discussed them with his brother Hernando and his officers. His plight grew even worse, for the Indians stole out of the forest at night to destroy his food stores.

Suddenly, in the midst of this predicament, two sailing ships appeared on the sea to the north. They brought one hundred fresh infantrymen and cavalrymen commanded by a bold captain named Hernando de Soto. The sight of these soldiers,

with their shining armor and their prancing horses so cheered Pizarro and his men that they embarked almost at once for the conquest of Tumbez and its golden treasures.

Alas, as it happened they found only disappointment. Where Pizarro on his first trip had seen a city of white houses, and Indians in bright dresses going busily about in the streets, there was now but a plain of rubble over which stood the temple and the fortress, half-ruined and as forlorn as dead trees in a desert.

The soldiers' bitterness at the sight of these ruins soon turned to anger against their Captain.

"So this is what we have come for, some of us all the way from Spain. You promised us walls of gold and precious stones, gardens of golden flowers, but we find only sandy wastes, disease, mosquitoes and now this ruined city."

"We shall find the richer cities we have heard about," answered Pizarro.

"And they will be like this one. In ruin, stripped of their treasures."

"Let us not despair before we learn what happened to Tumbez," said Pizarro. "Perhaps it was an earthquake, or a war."

It was a civil war. So was the *curaca* of Tumbez and other Indians found hiding in the nearby woods.

"When our old Emperor Huayna Capac died," said the *curaca,* "he divided his country between his two sons, Atahuallpa and Huascar. That was sometime before you first came to out city. Atahuallpa ruled the north from his city of Quito. Huascar ruled the south from the beautiful capital of Cuzco. For a while, they were at peace. But Atahuallpa became unhappy reigning over but half of his father's realm. He wanted to be an Emperor as powerful as his father. So he led his great armies against his brother.

"It was a long war. Many fine towns were demolished, many people were killed. Atahuallpa vanquished his brother's armies and is now Emperor of all his father's realm. His brother is his prisoner, but many of Huascar's soldiers still want to fight for their king, and so one may say that the war is not yet ended. But Tavantinsuyu now needs peace."

"Tavantinsuyu?" asked Pizarro.

"Yes. That is the name of our country. It means the Four Corners of the World."

"So that is the name of the Land of Gold,' said Pizarro. "We have also called it Peru. Long ago near Panama, an Indian told of a country to the south which he called Peru or Biru. We thought that *it* was the Land of Gold."

"We do not know the name Peru," said the Indian.

"Well, that matters not," declared Pizarro, "for by the will of our King your country will henceforth be called New Castile."

The Indians wondered about that foreign King who was so great that he could rename their country and send across the seas soldiers who fought from the backs of big animals. But their own King was greater, they thought. Had he not larger armies, and was he not the descendent of the Sun-God, himself a god on earth? And they told the story of their Kings:

[*The legend* "There was a time, long, long, ago, when the people *of the sun*] of the country lived like the wild animals of the forest. They fed on berries, on the animals which they could kill, and even ate their enemies who had fallen in battle. They thought only of war.

"The Sun who had long contemplated their plight from his palace high in the sky, pitied them and decided to change their ways into those of civilized people. He called his son, the Inca, Manco Capac, and his daughter Mama Oello and, giving them a gold scepter, said to them:

" 'Descend upon the Earth with this scepter, and walk until it will, of itself, sink deep into the ground. In that place you will teach the people how to be happy and peaceful.'

"Manco Capac and Mama Oello obeyed their father and alighted near the lake Titicaca, high up in the mountains. They walked down the beautiful valleys until, suddenly, the scepter sprung from the hand of Manco and sank deep into the ground, like a stone falling into the water. Manco now called to this place all the wild men of the country, and with them began to build a city which they named Cuzco. When every man and woman had a house of his own, Manco taught them the art of ploughing the soil, of seeding corn, manioc, potatoes, beans and other grains and vegetables, while Mama Oello taught the women weaving, spinning and sewing, and the art of cooking.

"They had around them a happy and growing people who lived peacefully together. When Manco and Mama Oello died, Manco's son and all his descendants—the Incas—continued to reign over the people and to spread these arts and many others to the neighboring countries. Sometimes they did so peacefully, but there were times when people wanted to continue living in their own way and the Incas had first to conquer them. And thus the Incas became great warriors too, and the country over which they rule now is so large that it takes a balsa many weeks to sail along its shores."

The Indians told more about their country, and Pizarro marvelled at the richness and the power of the land he came to conquer.

Everything in Peru belonged to the Inca emperors. The mines whence came the gold, the silver, and the copper; the great llama herds tended by shepherds on the slopes of the mountains; the fields and the orchards, the houses, the lakes and the rivers. Each man, woman and child had to give part of his time for the Emperor and for the State. Some wove the beautiful embroidered clothes which the Spaniards had admired; some wrought the vases and jewelry of gold and silver; some built the temples and the Emperor's palaces; others mined the gold and the silver, or served in the armies of the Emperor. In season, all the people gathered to cultivate the fields for the Emperor, the Inca nobles, the priests of the Sun. The produce from the Emperor's fields went into great storehouses which were at all times filled with the things necessary to life.

The Emperor and his government used the wealth of the land and the labor of the people so well that no one in the realm lacked food, clothing and a house. When a man married—and every man was forced to take a wife—he was given a house to live in and enough ground in which to raise food for his family. If he lived in the mountains where it was cold, his wife was given the llama wool to spin and weave into warm clothes for her household; if he lived on the seashore where it was hot, his wife received cotton to make cool dresses. When he became sick or grew old his fields were cultivated for him. In time of drought when his fields gave him little, he received food from the Emperor's warehouses.

Fine roads were built all over the country so that one could travel comfortably from one end of the land to the other. Although there were no horses in Peru, and no carriages, a message from the Emperor could be carried swiftly to the farthest end of his empire. Small houses were built along the roads at short distances from one another; a runner carrying the Emperor's message ran only from one house to the next, and a second runner carried it to the third house, and so on.

The people of Peru were happy, but they were not free. Only the Emperor and his Inca nobles owned anything. No one could travel, move to another house, change trade, do anything, unless it was so ordered by the Emperor. If the Emperor furnished the wool for their dresses, he told his people what they must wear. But they were happy for they did not know what freedom was.

The Emperor lived amidst marvelous riches. His palace walls were decorated with animals and birds of gold and precious stones. His gardens were planted with flowers and vegetables made of gold. He ate and drank out of vessels of gold; he sat on seats of gold; he bathed in fountains of gold, and traveled on a couch of gold.

He was indeed a great Emperor, a God on Earth, the descendant of the Sun-God.

This was the country where there was as much gold as there is water in the sea.

One against Two Thousand

Pizarro and his soldiers thought a great deal about what the Indians had told them. The conqueror was glad to know that the Land of Gold was even richer than he had dreamed. And what pleased him most was the news about the two brother kings who made war upon each other. He remembered that his cousin Cortes could conquer Mexico because the Mexicans fought between themselves instead of fighting him. He was hopeful, but his soldiers were not.

"Just more of those wonderful stories," they said among themselves. "If we go on, we will have nothing but more wonderful stories, more disease, more fighting, and more ruined cities."

Those thoughts might well have led the men to revolt, but Pizarro ordered them to make ready and march on. "While they are busy," he said to his officers, "they will not think of groaning."

So the captain rode out of Tumbez at the head of his army to explore the country to the south and find a good place to build a town with a fort. From that town he would set out to look for the Emperor and in it he could find refuge should he be defeated in battle.

After searching for thirty days through the hot, dry country between the mountains and the sea, they came to a valley, so well planted with fruit trees and vegetable gardens that Pizarro decided at once that it was a suitable site for his town. It was near the sea, and the Spanish ships could sail up the streams that ran through it.

Pizarro, his soldiers, and the Indians whom they had forced into their service, soon were very busy. Some fetched stones and fitted them into walls, others cut down trees, sawed them into boards and beams and joined them to make roofs, floors, doors, and windows.

A Spanish town with a church, a fort, and a town hall began to rise on the soil of the Land of Gold. The Spaniards named it San Miguel. When it was nearly finished, Pizarro made ready to seek the Emperor. He gathered his men around him and said, "These past weeks I have watched the sea hoping that some ships from Panama would bring us more soldiers. They have not come and we can wait no longer. Those who are sick and weary, and have no heart for fighting, will remain to guard San Miguel. Let the rest be ready to follow me across the mountain passes to the valleys where Emperor Atahuallpa is said to be camping in the midst of his army. We may be one against two thousand but the victory will be the greater."

The captain told his men to make friends with the Indians. "That will be easy," he added, "because the Indians in those parts were ruled by good King Huascar before he lost his country to his brother, and they will want to see us fight Atahuallpa."

Some days later, Pizarro put on his helmet, buckled his armor, and left San Miguel followed by sixty cavalry men commanded by Hernando Pizarro and Hernando de Soto, seventy infantrymen with their pikes pointing up to the sky, twenty crossbowmen loaded down with arrows, three arquebusiers with their arquebuses, Pedro de Candia with a small cannon, and a long file of Indians bearing the baggage. Two priests rode along on horses, and the Indians who had gone to Spain

97

with Pizarro and were now his interpreters, trudged on with the infantry.

With the clanging of their arms and the thumping of their horses' hoofs, Pizarro and his army were off to conquer the Land of Gold.

They followed the green valleys which rose toward the mountain, and along the way they saw the industrious Indians hard at work in their fields or tending their llama herds. Sometimes they passed grey stone fortresses which looked down upon them from the top of high rocks, or they halted for a rest in some adobe town where stood the stone barracks of the Emperor's army. And all along the way they spread the news that they had come to avenge good King Huascar and so they were left in peace.

In many towns they saw the palaces in which the Emperor rested during his travels, and they marveled how unlike they were from the King of Spain's castles with their outside walls smooth and grey and almost windowless. More like boxes than palaces, they thought. But boxes of jewels. Indeed, the soldiers' eyes opened wide with greed at the sight of the precious treasures in their dark interiors.

But the fortresses and the palaces were empty and silent. Where were the Emperor's soldiers?

While the Spaniards were thus following their Captain deeper and deeper into Peru, they began to realize that it was perhaps a much more powerful country than Spain; and some of them grew fearful. Sensing this, Pizarro stopped in a pleasant valley sweet with the odor of unknown flowers and, rising in his stirrups, he spoke to his men: "We are now starting on the

most dangerous part of our adventure. If some of our companions do not have the heart to go forward, it is not too late for them to turn back. Too few soldiers guard San Miguel and it will be well if some men return to protect it. I will go forward only with those who do not hesitate to share the grave dangers ahead."

The soldiers considered his words. Most of them decided quickly.

"No retreat for us," they shouted to Pizarro. "We have come to see this adventure to the end. We shall follow you even to death."

But five cavalrymen and four infantrymen did not join in these shouts. "We have no taste for this journey to death," they muttered. "We will go back." With wishes of good luck to their comrades, they took the way to San Miguel.

"Now," said Pizarro, "I am rid of the faint-hearted. I can march on and will hear no more grumbling."

After days of trudging up cool mountains and down hot valleys where silent bats alighted at night upon the sleeping soldiers to suck their blood, they came in sight of a valley amidst mountains. It was like a garden enclosed within grey walls. Pointing to a town in the middle of the valley, Pizarro said to Hernando de Soto: "I will go and rest with the infantry in that town. In the meantime you go with the cavalry to scout the country ahead and find, if you can, the whereabouts of the Emperor's armies. I do not like the way he allows us to travel freely in his own land without attempting to fight us. He must have a trap set for us somewhere. As we have seen, in all the villages and towns young men have been called into his armies which must be very great indeed. But where are they?"

At this Hernando de Soto and his cavalry galloped away in a cloud of dust. The infantry moved on toward the town where many houses had been shattered during the war between the two Inca brothers.

Pizarro rested for a while among the Indians, waiting eagerly

for his horsemen and the news which they would bring. After a week had gone by, he became worried. Had De Soto fallen into an ambush in the mountain? But one morning the town resounded with the clatter of horse's hoofs. Hernando de Soto was back, not only with much news. With him was an Inca ambassador in a woolen robe studded with gold and precious stones. He was accompanied by Indians carrying twenty-five gifts from the Emperor: a model fortress made of baked clay, many embroidered woolens and some skinned ducks.

"My master, the Great Inca Emperor, bids you welcome. He invites you to visit him in his mountain camp," said the ambassador. Then he walked among the strange soldiers. He touched their arms to feel their strength. He patted their steel armor, and even pulled their beards to see if they were real. He also counted them. As Pizarro watched, he realized that the Emperor had sent the man only to determine the size of the Spanish army.

But Pizarro was as wily as the Emperor. He presented the

ambassador with a red cap, a linen shirt, and two glass cups. "These are presents for your Emperor from my own King, who is the greatest on earth," he said. "And tell him that we are ready to help him fight all his enemies."

The ambassador departed, pleased to have counted so few soldiers. But he had also seen sixty of the strange animals on which the bearded soldiers rode when they fought.

Hernando de Soto then told of his trip and about the towns farther into the mountains. "They are more beautiful than the ones we have seen," he said. "We saw buildings where shoes and clothing for the Emperor's army are stored. And others where women make wine for the soldiers. The deeper we go into the country the more evidence we find of wealth. The Indians are better gardeners than the Spanish peasants; they cultivate gardens even on the slopes of mountains, and the walls they build to keep the soil and the water from running down make the mountains look like giant stairways."

"But where is the Emperor and his army?" asked Pizarro.

"The Emperor has more than one army. One is still fighting the soldiers of King Huascar; another, we heard, is encamped on a plain on the far side of the mountain. There the Emperor waits for us. This country is so great that it seems foolhardy to think that we can conquer it."

Pizarro ignored de Soto's misgivings and ordered his men to pack their belongings. They were soon tramping forward. For a while their trip was made easy by a beautiful road of stone paving shaded by trees planted on either side. But soon they were stopped by a river so wide that they had to build a floating bridge of logs to cross it. On the opposite shore, Indians greeted

them with bad news. The Emperor, they were told, was waiting with three armies on the other side of the mountain near a town called Caxamalca. Another army was guarding the mountain passes and using for a flag a shirt that Pizarro had sent the Emperor. Yet, a little farther on, other Indians said that the Emperor was not waiting there, but was marching with fifty thousand men in the country to the south.

In this quandary Pizarro did what the Emperor had done. He sent an ambassador—one of the Indian interpreters—to find the Emperor and to count his soldiers. As the ambassador walked swiftly away, the troops resumed their march and presently arrived at the foot of the blue mountains which Pizarro had seen from his ship. They rose, rock upon rock, until their summits pierced the clouds. The soldiers shivered at the thought of climbing so high; they glanced with envy at the smooth road bordered by trees which wound away to the south.

Seeing that his men hesitated, Pizarro raised his hand toward the mountains and shouted: "This, I believe, is the best way to approach the Emperor; to try any other way would be to show him that we are afraid. Take heart and go forward like good soldiers. At the hour of the gravest danger our God will protect us. He will help us bring to the unbelievers the knowledge of our faith, and to win their country for our King."

"Lead on!" shouted the soldiers. "Lead on! We will follow you and show you what we can do in the cause of our God and our King."

After a night's rest, they began to climb. Pizarro led the way as always while his brother Hernando commanded the rear; the cavalrymen led their horses by the bridles; the infantry

puffed under their heavy armor; the Indians moaned with the weight of the baggage on their backs. Like a long serpent they wound their way up the steep paths cut into the mountain wall. They crawled across swinging bridges thrown over the cracks in the rocks, and squeezed through narrow gorges where the torrents rumbled.

Pizarro looked cautiously about when they passed by the stone fortresses that stood guard over the path. But they were always empty and silent. The Spaniards even spent the night in one of them to protect themselves against the icy wind.

Even though they watched every rock and every crack for the sight of an Indian as they continued upward, they saw only the wild vicuñas jumping about the slopes, and the condors gliding over the summits. The Emperor, it appeared, was not planning to attack them in the mountain passes.

But surely Atahuallpa was aware of their progress, for one evening on the highest pass, as they warmed themselves with bright fires, another ambassador came to bring them greetings and some llama meat from the Emperor. And yet a third ambassador came two days later as they were about to begin the descent on the other side of the mountain. He too brought the warm greetings of the Emperor and more presents.

"The Emperor," he said "wants to show you his good will even before you reach his camp in the plain of Caxamalca."

"He must be very impatient to cut off our heads," thought Pizarro. "But we must not let him know our suspicions." He said to the ambassador, "We are even more eager to show the Emperor our friendship for him, and to tell him about our own greater King and our God, the true one."

It was at this moment that Pizarro's own ambassador arrived and made quite a scene.

"Do not treat these dogs better than their Emperor treated me," he cried pointing to the Inca nobleman. "Atahuallpa would not see me and I barely escaped with my head. The Emperor lured you across the mountain to kill you and your soldiers. His soldiers lay in wait in greater numbers than the stones on this mountain path. He has ordered all the inhabitants out of the town of Caxamalca so that they will not hinder his soldiers in the hour of battle."

"This man lies," answered the Emperor's ambassador. "My Emperor's intentions toward you are those of a friend."

Pizarro said that he did not doubt the Emperor's friendship for him, and ordered his troops to start down the mountain.

They were more than halfway down when a beautiful sight presented itself. A deep green valley spread down below covered with fields and orchards divided by streams and canals. In the center, the houses of Caxamalca shone like jewels on a velvet gown. It seemed a paradise to the soldiers, but they were disheartened by what they saw in the distance. There the white tents of Atahuallpa's army were spread in orderly rows so large that it would have taken a man almost a day to walk around it. Amidst the tents, set in a grove of trees, stood the palace of the Emperor.

The soldiers' heart sank low at the sight. They would have been happy to turn back, but their old captain spurred his horse and, with banners flying, they followed him down the mountain. They arrived at the deserted city of Caxamalca just as hail and rain began to fall.

No living things peeped from behind the painted brick walls as the Spaniards tramped down the wet streets. In the great plaza of the town, only the clattering of the rain on the roofs greeted them. Pizarro, ever on his guard for a surprise attack, ordered his men to stop in the middle of the plaza while he went to investigate the stone fortress which stood at one end.

Atahuallpa

Instead of waiting for the Emperor to come now, Pizarro decided to make the first move. He ordered Hernando de Soto and fifteen horsemen to go into the Emperor's camp to see what sort of an army he had and what his plans were. Then, fearing that de Soto might be in danger with so few men he sent his brother Hernando after him with fifteen more men.

With trumpets blowing and swords clanging against their armor, the cavaliers whizzed past the Emperor's soldiers who stood like statues between rows and rows of tents, and came to a halt in the courtyard of the white palace which they had seen from the mountain. All the courtiers of the Emperor were assembled, their brilliantly colored robes and their heavy gold earrings sparkling even in the grey weather.

When de Soto came closer, he saw, sitting on a gold stool among the noblemen, an Inca in a plain robe and a red fringed scarf around his head. It was Atahuallpa, the great Emperor who ruled over the country where there was as much gold as there was water in the sea. The scarf around his head was the *borla*, the symbol of his power.

De Soto bowed on his horse and made a great sweep with

his cap. "Oh, great Emperor," he said, "I am the subject of a powerful King across the sea. We have come because we have heard of your wonderful victories and want to offer you the service of our arms and to impart to you the knowledge of our God. My chief, the captain who has led us here, greets you and should be pleased to receive your visit in Caxamalca."

De Soto might as well have spoken to a deaf and blind person.

Fortunately Hernando Pizarro rode up at this moment.

"Will Your Majesty tell us what he wishes us to do for him?" he asked.

At last the Emperor, without looking up, said: "Tell your captain that I shall visit him tomorrow with my generals and my army. Tell him to live, in the meantime, in the houses on the plaza, no others. When I come, I will order what shall be done."

As he was saying that, de Soto's horse began to prance and paw the ground with such impatience that the Emperor could not help looking at the beautiful animal. Hernando de Soto directly saw his chance to show what a good horseman he was. He spurred the animal and galloped off between the rows of tents, then turned around and around, frightening the Indian soldiers who stood in his path. Finally he galloped back at furious speed and halted before the Emperor.

Atahuallpa remained as still as a stone, but later he ordered his officers to cut off the heads of all the soldiers who had stepped back in fear.

Young Indian girls in striped robes brought wine in gold cups, and the Spaniards after toasting the Emperor, rode

through the long rows of tents and away toward Caxamalca to report to Pizarro the great power of Emperor Atahuallpa.

That night, the Spanish soldiers sat gloomily about the plaza of Caxamalca watching the Inca campfires which sparkled like the stars over the distant hills.

"Tomorrow the Emperor will come and put us all to death," said one of the soldiers. "He decoyed us across the mountains with his gifts and greetings so that he could trap us in this empty town."

"And we cannot flee," said a cavalryman whose armor reflected the fire. "Over the mountain passes the Inca soldiers will wait for us."

Pizarro, alone, had no fear. He tried to comfort his men, and even devised a plan to snare the Emperor in his own trap. This plan he discussed with his officers part of the night, then he placed sentries on the highest wall of the fortress and around the town and waited for daybreak.

It was a long wait and no one really slept. The Captain thought of his plan. The soldiers, huddled against one another, watched for the stars to fade in the morning light. When the trumpet finally sounded the troops gathered shivering with cold and fear to hear Pizarro's orders for the day, their gravest day.

Pizarro divided his cavalry forces into two groups, one commanded by Hernando Pizarro, the other by Hernando de Soto. They were, he told them, to hide with their horses in certain of the houses that lined the plaza. They were also to tie bells to the breastplates of their horses. The infantry, he also divided, indicating for their hiding places, the houses on the other side of the square. As for Pedro de Candia and the trumpeteers he sent them to wait in the fortress with the falconet.

"Now," the Captain explained, "you shall remain in hiding until the Inca Emperor comes into the plaza. When I wave my white scarf, that will be the signal for Pedro de Candia to fire the falconet and for all the rest of you to rush out of hiding and fall upon the Indian soldiers in the plaza and put them to flight. I think in this way we will take them by surprise. They will be too frightened by the sudden attack to fight. That is our only hope. As for the Emperor, we must take him alive. If we hold him prisoner, I think we shall be saved."

They all knelt down while the priest prayed to the white man's God for help.

And then they went into hiding.

It was well after midday when the sentinels on the wall of the fortresses announced that the Inca army was coming out of its camp.

Pizarro climbed to the top of the fortress. What he saw was as magnificent as it was frightening.

Like the incoming tide the Inca hordes were rolling over the valley toward Caxamalca. They were led by hundreds and hundreds of Indians in multi-colored shirts who were sweeping the road where the Emperor was to pass. Behind them were troops of men and women dressed in red and white checkered robes, who danced and sang of the power and the prowess of the Emperor. Then, riding over the heads of the Indians like a ship upon the sea, came Atahuallpa's gold litter carried by Inca nobles clothed in sky-blue robes sprinkled with gold and emeralds. All around the litter, and for a long distance behind, marched crowds of guards in white dresses with gold maces in their hands. On each side of the road, covering the meadows as far as the eye could see, the Inca soldiers came marching, armed with spears, bows and arrows, slings and clubs.

It all glittered so that Pizarro's eyes were almost blinded when he climbed down from the fortress.

As the Indians came slowly on, the songs grew louder and louder, sounding more and more to the Spaniards like a warning that their end was near.

The singing and the dancing continued until the Incas entered Caxamalca, and the host of road sweepers opened into two long rows on each side of the plaza. Then, there was a deep silence while the Emperor, from the center of the plaza, looked around in amazement at not seeing the Spaniards. Pizarro from his hiding place noticed with relief that almost all the soldiers had remained outside the town walls. There were several thousand Indians in the plaza, but these did not seem to be armed except for the gold maces which some carried.

"Where are the strangers?" demanded Atahuallpa.

One of the Spaniards, a priest, presently stepped out into the plaza with a crucifix in one hand and a Bible in the other, and an Indian interpreter walking behind him.

"I am coming by order of my commander," said the priest stopping in front of the litter, "to talk to you about our God." He told Atahuallpa the story of Christ and his apostles; the story of the Popes who, he said, ruled over all the kings of

the earth. "That is why," he continued, "our King Charles has sent Captain Francisco Pizarro to this country; to make you and your people renounce your own false gods and accept the faith of the Christians, which is the true one; and to see that you become subjects of the King of Spain."

Emperor Atahuallpa frowned at this discourse, and his black eyes flared with anger. "I do not understand much of what you say," he answered. "But I know that if you have come to change my faith, you have also come to take my country and steal our gold. I will be the subject of no other man for I am the greatest prince on earth. Your king may be great. I do not doubt it when I see that he sends his captains so far across the sea; but he must be mad to talk of a country which does not belong to him as if it were his own. As for my faith, I will not change it. "My god," and Atahuallpa pointed up to the setting sun, "shines up in heaven, and looks down upon his children. Besides," the Emperor continued, "what gives you the right to say these things?"

"This book," answered the priest, handing the Bible to Atahuallpa.

The Inca Emperor opened it and looked at it for a while. He did not understand it, but, suddenly he threw the book to the ground and cried: "Tell your captain and his soldiers that they shall give me an account of all the crimes that they have committed in my land. I will not go from here till they have given back all that they have stolen and repaired all the wrongs they have done."

The priest indignantly picked up the Bible and hurried to tell Pizarro what Atahuallpa had said and done.

The time to strike had come.

Pizarro waved his scarf. From the fortress the falconet thundered and the trumpet sounded; from the houses around the plaza the cavaliers with their horses' bells ringing, and the infantrymen, with their pikes forward burst out bellowing their war cries, "Sant Iago and at them!" And they all fell upon the terrified Indians. Trampled down under the horses' feet, deafened by the booms of the falconet and of the arquebuses and the blowing of the trumpets, blinded by the smoke, cut and pierced by swords and pikes, the poor Indians tried to flee from the plaza. But the entrance was too narrow for all of them to pass through at once, so they threw themselves against the town walls on one side of the plaza, and, when it broke down, they poured out of the city like water from a broken dam.

Many Inca nobles remained to defend their Emperor. As those who carried the litter were killed, others took their places. The litter was never let down. Some cavalrymen, at last, angered at not being able to reach the Emperor were preparing to kill him with their swords when Pizarro galloped to the rescue yelling: "Let no man wound the Emperor on pain of death." Then, with the help of some of his men, he took the Inca Emperor off his throne, and led him into the largest house on the plaza.

The great Emperor Atahuallpa was a prisoner.

His own soldiers, who stood in the plain outside the city walls trying to understand the catastrophe which had befallen them, were filled with panic when the news of Atahuallpa's capture reached them. They never even thought of fighting. The bearded strangers who had dared lay their hands upon the Child of the Sun were not mere men, to be sure. They were gods too; one does not fight gods. Besides, who could lead them now? Atahuallpa was in the hands of the strangers and King Huascar was a prisoner of Atahuallpa's captains. And so, as night fell, the plain was filled with disconsolate soldiers who wandered about, not knowing what to do, yet not wanting to leave the place where their Emperor was held. The next day, they went back to their homes as Pizarro ordered.

The rude Spaniards really did not comprehend their easy victory. Not one of them was wounded, except Pizarro whose hand was slashed by the swords of his own soldiers when he saved the Emperor's life. How their situation had changed! In the morning they had feared that their last day had come. Now they were to be masters in the Land of Gold.

That evening, Pizarro dined with Atahuallpa. But it was no longer the proud Inca Emperor who sat with him at the dinner table. It was a sad man who wondered what devil dwelled inside these terrible strangers who had so treacherously attacked him.

No doubt, Atahuallpa had thought that so few men would not dare touch the mighty Emperor in the midst of his army. He had been confident that he was master of the situation; he would decide whether to treat them as friends or as enemies. That is why he had left the greatest part of his army outside the city. And now *he* was trapped. If only he had known how wicked and clever these strangers were, he would have destroyed them as they crossed the mountain passes, or even as they landed in his country. But, alas, it was too late.

Nevertheless, he still had hope. He knew well the Spaniards' greed for gold; it gave him an idea. The next day he asked that Pizarro come to his room.

"If you let me go free," he said, "I will give you enough gold to fill this room, as high as I can reach."

"And that is not all," Atahuallpa went on. "I will fill with silver the next room which is even larger. I will fill it twice! My people will bring these treasures from all over my land. I ask four months to accomplish this."

Pizarro gazed at Atahuallpa, hardly believing him. The room was immense; two ships loaded to the water line would be needed to carry so much gold. Atahuallpa in turn looked at Pizarro waiting for an answer.

"I must not remain a prisoner too long," thought Atahuallpa. "These strangers have said that they were on the side of

Huascar, and they will deliver him from my captains. They will make him the Emperor and rule my land through him."

"Should I free Atahuallpa?" wondered Pizarro. "His offer will afford us a quick way of gathering gold; his people will probably hide their gold as they have already done in some places. I can lose nothing by saying yes. By the time this marvelous treasure is here I will have made Huascar the Emperor. Atahaullpa will be less dangerous then."

So Pizarro said yes. At once a red line was traced on the wall to show the place where Atahuallpa's hand had reached, and the agreement was carefully drawn up. Then Atahuallpa gave orders to his loyal servants to depart for all parts of the land to gather the treasure.

Atahuallpa now set about living like an emperor in the house where the Spaniards had put him. Pizarro ordered his soldiers to treat him with the respect due such a great sovereign. His family and servants were permitted to stay with him and his courtiers allowed to visit him. Every day, the noble Incas with the heavy ear pendants came to kiss his feet, leaving their shoes and entering Atahuallpa's room with a heavy weight upon their shoulders. That was the way in Tavantinsuyu to show one's humility in the presence of the Emperor.

The wardrobe of Atahuallpa was brought to Caxamalca. Often he liked to wear mantles woven with the wool of the wild vicuña, a wool so much finer than the llama's that no one but the Emperor could have dresses made of it. At other times he wore mantles made from the skins of bats which were even softer than vicuña wool or the feathers of tropical birds.

For a hat, Atahuallpa always put on the *llautu*, a small turban made of woolen braids of many colors, and over it, even though he was a prisoner, he still wore the *borla*, which was to the Inca Emperors what the gold crown was to the ancient kings of Europe.

Atahuallpa specially liked to change his dress when he was about to take his meals, squatted in front of a low table covered with rushes where the dishes of gold were placed. If he happened to spill a little food on his dress, he would leave the room at once and return in a new dress to finish his meal. The soiled dress was never washed. It was placed in a great chest with other clothing and things which he had tired of using. Every so often the contents of the chest were burned, for no one, on pain of death, could use the things which the Emperor had touched.

Thus Atahuallpa was still living the part of an Emperor.

In the meantime, the treasure began to arrive, borne upon the shoulders of Indian porters. Never had the Spaniards dreamed of so much gold. Almost daily new things were added to the piles of gold and silver. There were plates, cups, salvers, vases, beautifully carved by skilled craftsmen; there was a gold fountain; there were llamas, jaguars, ducks, and other animals and birds from the Emperor's palaces; flowers, vegetables, and ears of corn, which ornamented his gardens; there were big tiles and slabs from the floors and walls of the temples in Cuzco and other cities. The Spaniards saw only the gold in all these treasures; the art with which they were wrought was lost upon them.

Being brought from far away places, the treasures arrived

too slowly for the Spaniards who were impatient to receive their share and go on to conquer the rest of the Land of Gold. Atahuallpa, too, became impatient; he wanted to be freed. He worried lest Huascar be brought to Caxamalca, a thing which he dreaded so much that, one day, he made up his mind to do away with him. "If Huascar were no more," he thought, "the Spanish Captain would have to deal with him, Atahuallpa. So he confided his wish to some loyal officers who went to the town where Huascar was imprisoned, and drowned him in a nearby river.

But this cruel deed worked ill for Atahuallpa.

Pizarro knew that Huascar, grateful to be delivered, and a gentle prince, would have agreed to rule the country under him, thus making it safe for the Spaniards. But it was not so with Atahuallpa. He was a bellicose lord who wanted to avenge himself for the insults and the treacherous attack of the strangers. If he were freed, he would soon lead his armies against them; and there were many armies still roaming through the land waiting for orders from the only leader they had left. Thus Pizarro was in a quandary and Atahuallpa had made it almost impossible for the Captain to free him.

Things became even worse for Atahuallpa when rumors spread that his generals, on secret orders from him, were preparing to attack Caxamalca with big armies. Hernando Pizarro who went to scout the country found these rumors false, but, nevertheless, the Spaniards were worried. If Atahuallpa gave such orders, it might go badly for them, isolated as they were in this big country.

The news that Diego de Almagro was coming and was crossing the passes in the mountain with one hundred and fifty men did not reassure them entirely.

"Let's divide the treasure now," the soldiers demanded, "so that each of us can have his share. Then we can leave this city and march through the rest of the country to make sure that it is really ours."

Finding this request reasonable, Pizarro agreed to divide the treasure although the rooms were not yet full. It was the

biggest ransom that a king had ever paid. The King of Spain's share was put aside first, and Hernando Pizarro was sent to Spain with it to insure its safe arrival. The rest was divided among the soldiers, the cavalrymen receiving the largest share. All the beautiful plates, animals, vases, and flowers were then melted into ingot to be sent for safekeeping to San Miguel.

But what was to be done with Atahuallpa since he could not be freed safely?

Most of the Spaniards wanted to put him to death. "Hasn't he killed his brother Huascar?" they asked.

The others were indignant at this demand. Hernando de Soto who had become Atahuallpa's friend was among them. "It would be a perfidy to do so," he cried angrily. "Hasn't he kept his promise? If it is not safe for us to free him, then let us take him to Spain where he will be well treated. I offer to accompany him."

Pizarro said nothing. He thought that they would be much safer if Atahuallpa were condemned to die, but he knew that it woud be a treacherous act, indeed, and he would rather have his soldiers take the blame for it. That is why he let the majority have their way, and, after a short judgment, Atahuallpa was put to death. And that was the end of the last great Inca Emperor, whose country had as much gold as there was water in the sea.

The Inca generals were now left without a leader. They became so divided that they lost all heart for the fight against the clever bearded men. Only one Inca really found the will and the boldness to fight the Spaniards. He was Manco, the young brother of Huascar. After learning the white men's ways of fighting, he almost succeeded in chasing them from his country. But it was too late. Tavantinsuyu, the Land of Gold, had been won for the King of Spain.

The dream of the young swineherd had come true; old Francisco Pizarro had become the Conqueror of Peru.